AMERICAN EXPORT LINES
UNITED STATES LINES

BRITISH OCEAN LINERS

A twilight era, 1960–85

ORSOVA

BRITISH OCEAN LINERS

A twilight era, 1960-85

WILLIAM MILLER

PSL Patrick Stephens, Wellingborough

First published in 1986

British Library Cataloguing in Publication Data

Miller, William H. (William Henry)
British liners
1. Ocean liners—Great Britain—History—20th century
I. Title
387.2′43 HE566.025

ISBN 0-85059-766-8

Patrick Stephens Limited is part of the Thorsons Publishing Group

Photoset in 10 on 11pt Garamond by Avocet Marketing Services, Bicester, Oxon. Printed in Great Britain on 115gsm Fineblade coated cartridge, and bound by Oxford University Press, Oxford, for the publishers, Patrick Stephens Limited, Denington Estate, Wellingborough, Northants, NN8 2QD, England.

Contents

Acknowledgements 6
Preface 7
Introduction 8
Far-flung services 9
Accommodation 12
The passengers 13
Cruising 14
Withdrawal and decline 18

Steamship companies
Anchor Line 21
Bibby Line 22
Blue Funnel Line 25
Blue Star Line 30
Booth Line 33
British India Steam Navigation Company Ltd 34
Canadian Pacific 48
Cunard Line 51
Curnow Shipping Ltd 72
Donaldson Line 73
Elder Dempster Lines 74
Elders & Fyffes Ltd 76
Ellerman & Bucknall Line 78
Ellerman's Wilson Line 79
Furness Bermuda Line 80
Furness Warren Line 82
Glen Line 83
Henderson Line 86
New Zealand Shipping Company Ltd 86
P&O-Orient Lines and P&O Cruises Ltd 90
Pacific Steam Navigation Company Ltd 110
Princess Cruises 110
Royal Mail Lines 114
Shaw Savill Line 116
Union Castle Line 122
Bibliography 133
Index of passenger ships 134

Acknowledgements

Being a book containing a considerable number of photographs, many of them quite difficult to obtain, the author would like to note the very special assistance and cooperation of three individuals: Messrs Alex Duncan and Roger Sherlock, both master photographers and major international resources of passenger ship pictures, and Mr Stephen Rabson, who is the most helpful keeper of the giant P&O Group photo archives in London.

Other invaluable contributions and support came from Captain Eric Ashton Irvine, formerly with Cunard; Frank Braynard, curator of the Museum of the American Merchant Marine; photographers J. K. Byass, Michael Cassar and Luis Miguel Correia; Susan Alpert and the Cunard Line in New York; the Hapag Lloyd Shipyards at Bremerhaven; another fine photographer, Michael D. J. Lennon; Richard K. Morse; Thomas Young and the Port Authority of New York & New Jersey; two further marine photographers, B. Reeves and Fred Rodriguez; and from the enormous collections of Victor Scrivens, James L. Shaw, Everett Viez and the World Ship Society Photo Library.

Special thanks to all others for their participation and especially to Patrick Stephens Limited for accepting this project.

Preface

As a schoolboy in the late '50s and early '60s, watching from a New Jersey waterfront perch just across from the famed liner berths of New York City, few ships held more excitement and magic for me than the Cunarders. It didn't matter whether it was the majestic *Queen Mary*, the last of the three-stackers, or the smaller *Parthia*, a combination passenger and cargo ship. They were all wonderfully handsome, superb examples of ocean liner design and evocative hints of far-off shores. A highlight of any day spent along the harbour, staring across at the ships in their berths or seeing them as they passed before me, was to see those orange-red and black stacks. They always appeared brighter and larger and even higher than those aboard other ships. My imagination was certainly sparked.

Later, I would cross the Hudson and visit the grand Cunard offices at the lower end of Broadway. I would return laden with brochures, postcards and sailing schedules, and not only for their own ships, but for others such as British India, Orient Line and P&O. The Cunard family of ships seemed to be my link to those other, far more distant British-flag liners. From early Laurence Dunn books, I learned of these other ships in greater detail.

25 years ago, the British liner fleet was the largest on earth. Now, quite sadly, most of these ships and some of the firms that ran them are gone. They have been forced off the sealanes by a variety of heavy-handed factors: changing world politics, the intrusion of aircraft, faster and more efficient methods of cargo shipping, and staggering increases in fuel and labour costs. There are over 160 ships listed amidst these pages, but only a dozen or so still sail in British-flag service.

These liners—from the brilliant Cunard *Queens* and Canadian Pacific's *Empresses* to Royal Mail's *Andes* and Shaw Savill's *Dominion Monarch* and to Blue Funnel's little *Gorgon* and Ellerman Wilson's *Borodino*—are all part of a great cast of characters. The purpose of this book is to tell of this cast, the final members of a long-playing production, which has spanned the growth and then the decline of the British Empire. Listed are their dimensions and construction details, their types of machinery and the numbers of passengers they carried per class, and then, of course, a brief chronology of their careers. The final notations might be the most interesting to many readers. To those frequently asked inquiries, it offers some answers to 'whatever became of the . . . ?' In fact, they have met all sorts of endings: Shaw Savill's *Akaroa* class being converted to car carriers, no less; Elder Dempster's *Aureol* still serving as a hotel-ship in the Middle East; two of the Ellerman *City* liners transformed into Mediterranean ferries; the grand *Queen Mary* living in semi-retirement as a floating hotel and museum in southern California; her running-mate, the first *Elizabeth*, pathetically destroyed by fire in Hong Kong waters; the renowned *Caronia* hideously smashed into three pieces by a Pacific storm; and even the relatively new *Cunard Ambassador* which, following a fire, plied Eastern waters carrying sheep instead of passengers.

Numerous others, possibly more mercifully, went to the scrapyards—reduced to rubble (and memories) in a matter of weeks at some lonely Far Eastern backwater. Some of their remains, however, have found unlikely homes: furnishings from the *Caronia* serve in a New York City restaurant, mounted deck plans from the *Edinburgh Castle* adorn a Hawaiian luncheon club and a life-ring from the *Nevasa* decorated a wall of a San Francisco antique shop.

These are the final members of the last great British ocean liner fleet. They are worthy of at least one more loving look.

William H. Miller
Jersey City, New Jersey
December 1984

Introduction

In 1960, shipyards at Birkenhead, Barrow-in-Furness and Belfast were at work on the three largest British passenger liners since the *Queen Elizabeth* of 1940. Union-Castle was adding the 37,600-ton *Windsor Castle*, the biggest ever for the South African trade, while the recently merged P&O and Orient lines were awaiting the greatest team intended for service other than the North Atlantic, the 41,900-ton *Oriana* and the 45,700-ton *Canberra.* Press reports could hardly ignore the obvious excitement. The immediate future seemed bright: Canadian Pacific looked to their *Empress of Canada*, Shaw Savill had the *Northern Star* on order and Union Castle planned yet another major ship, the *Transvaal Castle*. Most notably, however, Cunard was talking seriously of a 75,000-tonner to replace the ageing *Queen Mary*. There seemed to be enormous hope and encouraging promise for the British passenger fleet, then the largest and most widespread in the world.

These ships formed a new, contemporary generation and appeared to be only very distant relatives to their earlier, far more traditional predecessors. The towering upper decks of the *Windsor Castle* were to be capped by a single domed funnel and mast above the wheelhouse. She would not resemble the long familiar Castle liners, such as the *Capetown Castle* and subsequent *Pretoria Castle*, with their wide, flat stacks and twin tall masts. The *Oriana* had a single, top-deck stack, a second device that appeared to be a stack (it was a ventilator), but which was placed on a lower, uneven level, and then a single stump mast forward. She was quite different from the Orient Line's previous flagship, the *Orsova.* P&O's *Canberra* was perhaps the most revolutionary. Her most forward decks were rounded and rose to a single mast. Far aft, leaving a very clean midships space, were twin, raked uptakes—not even the customary funnel. She hardly seemed to come from the same fleet that had built the *Straths, Himalaya* and *Arcadia.*

Years earlier, most notably at the end of the Second World War, British designers began to take innovative, often bold steps in ocean liner design. In the process, they produced some of the finest and most successful passenger ships ever built. Even so, there was often a noticeable design element that could be linked to a firm's pre-war tonnage.

The Orient Line—particularly noted for producing a pair of very handsome ships, the *Orion* and *Orcades* of 1935–37—took the overall design of these ships, the latter of which had been lost in the war, for their new post-war replacement trio. The *Orcades* of 1948 used the general hull and superstructure forms of the earlier ships, but then, in a strong bid at the future, innovatively had her short mast and funnel grouped closely together and placed above the bridge and wheelhouse. Such a style had never been seen before. It was most effective and, with only slight modification, was used on the *Oronsay* of 1951. Three years later, the company went a step further: They eliminated the single, short mast entirely and used the large funnel as the new *Orsova*'s centrepiece and attachment for rigging.

Cunard also sought innovation in the late '40s. The company's previous ships, the *Mauretania* of 1939 and the *Queen Elizabeth* of 1940, were indeed very handsome, but in the classical tradition: twin funnels placed between twin masts. For their next large liner, the silhouette was to be far different, however. Twin funnels were replaced by one, very wide stack. The two masts were eliminated and replaced by a very tall, tripod creation, that was also—like the Orient Line ships—placed above the bridge. Furthermore, even the colouring was to be different. Instead of the customary black hull, white superstructure and upperworks, shades of green were used. There were, of course, heat resistant qualities in such colouring (especially important as the new liner was intended to spend considerable time on tropical cruise voyages), but it was also a huge bid at originality, an effort to create a highly recognisable, separate identity for the new *Caronia*. Almost immediately, she had a popular nickname, 'the Green Goddess'.

Some major companies opted to continue very closely with established pre-war designs. P&O's *Himalaya* (1949) and *Chusan* (1950) were clearly based on the *Stratheden* and her three surviving sisters from the '30s. Union-Castle's *Edinburgh Castle* and *Pretoria Castle* (both 1948) had only the slightest modifications from the *Capetown Castle* of a decade earlier. Others used traditional designs for their new post-war ships as well. Cunard's *Media* and *Parthia*, New Zealand Shipping Company's *Rangitane, Rangitoto* and *Ruahine*, and Ellerman's *City of Port Elizabeth* quartet were based certainly on standardised, large cargo ship plans, but then merely extended and reworked with significant passenger accommodation. Ships with lesser capacities, such as Bibby's *Leicestershire* and *Warwickshire*, the eight near-sisters for Blue Funnel and the foursome of the *Athenic* class for Shaw Savill, were even more noticeably of an enlarged cargo-liner type. Ships such as the *Jason* and *Ceramic* were subsequently duplicated by their owners, and well into the '50s, although limited only to the more customary dozen or so passenger berths.

During that post-war decade of British passenger ship rebuilding and renewal, the highest praises might well go to Shaw Savill's extraordinary *Southern Cross* of 1955. She was the first major ocean liner to have her engines, and therefore her funnel, placed well aft. Most significantly, this created substantial midships deck spaces and left the lower deck public rooms and passenger spaces free of cumbersome obstructions, such as shafts to the funnel and ventilating ducts. The *Southern Cross* began a revolutionary, highly successful style of design, one that attracted considerable attention and which was soon copied by the Dutch for their new transatlantic flagship *Rotterdam*, by P&O for their superb *Canberra* and was even repeated by Shaw Savill, some seven years later, for their *Northern Star* of 1962.

Until the early '60s, Britain had not only the world's largest passenger ship fleet, but her shipyards also created the greatest number of new liners, ships that were very often in the forefront of marine design and technology.

Almost without exception, the steamship firms mentioned in these pages come from the heyday of the British Empire, from that vast network of political, economic and social ties that spread to nearly every corner of the earth. Until the advent of the jet and the simultaneous dissolution of British overseas territories, in the 1950s and '60s, ships—especially passenger-cargo ships—were the vital links. Along their decks and in their lounges went the representatives of the Crown—the ministers, governors, adminstrators and civil servants, the police and troops, the scientists and technicians, the traders, missionaries, the families, the tourists and even the occasional member of the Royal Family. When these ties were severed, and some were cut quite abruptly, that steady, guaranteed flow of traffic, both in passenger and freight, ended. Without their livelihood, their economic well being, these ships—the last of a long breed under the British flag—disappeared, as did some of the firms themselves.

Far-flung services

There were very few mentionable ports in the world that were not visited by British passenger ships. The possible connections were enormous— from overnight crossings on the North Sea to nine weeks around Africa to 100 or more days travelling completely around the earth.

Perhaps the most famous and luxurious route was Cunard's transatlantic express, using the illustrious *Queen Mary* and *Queen Elizabeth*. Almost throughout the year, one of them would leave Southampton, usually on a Thursday, make a brief service call at Cherbourg for Continental passengers, and then head into the open Atlantic for the five-day, 28-knot passage to New York. They would arrive at the western end on the following Tuesday. It was a steady, convenient and precision relay—as the *Mary* left Southampton, the *Elizabeth* was already outward bound from New York. Ships such as the somewhat smaller and slower *Mauretania* offered support services, for the overflow of passengers mostly, on a slightly more extended run that crossed from Southampton to New York via Le Havre and Cobh.

Balanced, set schedules were very much a part of the North Atlantic run. Generally, it had the most established patterns of all worldwide liner services.

Other Cunarders, like the combination *Media* and *Parthia*, worked a monthly round-trip schedule between Liverpool and New York, and with just enough spare time for the occasional detour (prompted by freight demands mostly) to Greenock, Cobh, Bermuda or Norfolk. From eastern Canada, using the quartet of sisters *Saxonia*, *Ivernia*, *Carinthia* and *Sylvania*, there were twice-monthly sailings to Le Havre, Southampton and London and to Greenock and Liverpool. A sample Cunard sailing schedule from the late '50s illustrates these patterns:

Ship	From New York	Destination
Caronia	July 2	North Cape Cruise
Queen Mary	July 3	Cherbourg & Southampton
Media	July 5	Liverpool
Sylvania	July 5*	Greenock & Liverpool
Ivernia	July 5*	Le Havre & Southampton
Mauretania	July 10	Cobh, Le Havre & Southampton
Queen Elizabeth	July 11	Cherbourg & Southampton
Britannic	July 11	Cobh & Liverpool
Carinthia	July 12*	Liverpool
Queen Mary	July 17	Cherbourg & Southampton
Parthia	July 19	Liverpool
Saxonia	July 19*	Le Havre & Southampton
Scythia	July 25	Cobh & Liverpool
Sylvania	July 26*	Greenock & Liverpool
Ivernia	July 26*	Le Havre & Southampton
Mauretania	July 27	Cobh, Le Havre & Southampton
Queen Elizabeth	July 31	Cherbourg & Southampton

*These sailings were from Montreal.

Canadian Pacific with three liners, the *Empress of Britain, Empress of England* and *Empress of Canada*, ran a weekly timetable between Montreal, Quebec City, Greenock and Liverpool. An important ingredient of any successful passenger service was consistency in service, a set pattern of sailings that was well known and guaranteed. Even the less complex Furness Bermuda Line had an established schedule, sailing from New York to Bermuda almost every Saturday at three in the afternoon. Passengers could almost make reservations without consulting a sailing schedule.

On more long-distance services, such as to South America, there were well established patterns as well. Royal Mail's *Amazon, Aragon* and *Arlanza* sailed at three-week intervals, on their roundtrips from London and Cherbourg to Vigo, Lisbon, Las Palmas, Rio de Janeiro, Santos, Montevideo and Buenos Aires. The four sister-ships of Blue Star's *Argentina Star* class did the same, leaving the London Docks approximately every 21 days.

One of the most exact and specialised services was Union Castle's 'Cape Mail Express', from Southampton via either Madeira or Las Palmas and then on to Cape Town, Port Elizabeth, East London and Durban. Ship observers at Southampton often remarked that one's watch could be set by the accuracy of the weekly mailship sailings on Thursday afternoons at four. There was, until the mid '60s, a steady rotation of passenger mail liners, as indicated in this two-month listing from the spring of 1964:

Ship	From Southampton
Transvaal Castle	March 12
Capetown Castle	March 19
Pendennis Castle	March 26
Athlone Castle	April 2
Edinburgh Castle	April 9
Stirling Castle	April 16
Windsor Castle	April 23
Pretoria Castle	April 30
Transvaal Castle	May 7

Union Castle also ran nine-week round voyages that completely circled continental Africa, sailing from London and sometimes Rotterdam to Las Palmas, Ascension, St Helena, Walvis Bay, Cape Town, Port Elizabeth, Durban, Lourenco Marques, Beira, Dar-es-Salaam, Zanzibar, Tanga, Mombasa, Aden, Suez, Port Said, Genoa, Marseilles, Gibraltar and then homeward to London—or in reverse, going out via the East Coast ports first. Departures from London left every two weeks. When, in later years, Union Castle reduced its round-Africa fleet and then cut the service only to East Coast voyages that turned-around at Durban, the sailings of their last remaining ships were sensibly and efficiently coordinated with two one-time rivals on the same route, British India's *Kenya* and *Uganda*.

British India was another firm which maintained a vast passenger ship schedule. Aside from the East African run, to Port Said, Aden, Mombasa, Tanga, Zanzibar, Dar-es-Salaam and Beira, there was a connection from the same East African ports to Bombay—often via the Seychelles. At Bombay, there were sailings to the Persian Gulf as well as from across India, at Calcutta, to the Far East as far as Japan.

P&O–Orient offered sailing patterns and schedules that were the most diverse and far-flung of any passenger line, British or otherwise, especially after they reached heavily into the upper Pacific in the late '50s, going beyond their traditional Australia–New Zealand pattern, to the American West Coast and then transpacific to the Far East. The company accurately advertised that their ships 'spanned the globe'. There were very few ports that were not visited at least once or twice by one of the P&O–Orient liners.

A sample sailing schedule from the winter of 1965–66 reads as follows:

Ship	From the UK	Destinations
Oronsay	November 6	Le Havre, Lisbon, Trinidad, Cartagena, Cristobal, Acapulco, Los Angeles, San Francisco, Vancouver, Honolulu, Suva, Auckland, Sydney
Orsova	November 14	Gibraltar, Naples, Port Said, Aden, Bombay, Penang, Singapore, Fremantle, Adelaide, Melbourne, Sydney
Chusan	December 4	Madeira, San Juan, Port Everglades, Nassau, Cristobal, Acapulco, Los Angeles, San Francisco, Vancouver, Honolulu, Suva, Tonga, Auckland, Sydney
Oriana	December 5	Naples, Piraeus, Port Said, Aden, Colombo, Fremantle, Melbourne, Sydney
Orcades	January 1	Flushing, Port Said, Aden, Colombo, Fremantle, Adelaide, Melbourne, Wellington
Arcadia	January 13	Gibraltar, Port Said, Aden, Colombo, Fremantle, Melbourne, Sydney
Canberra	January 16	Naples, Port Said, Aden, Colombo, Fremantle, Melbourne, Sydney
Iberia	January 27	Gibraltar, Naples, Port Said, Aden, Bombay, Singapore, Fremantle, Melbourne, Sydney
Chitral	February 6	Port Said, Aden, Colombo, Penang, Port Swettenham, Singapore, Hong Kong, Kobe, Yokohama
Oriana	February 8	Gibraltar, Naples, Port Said, Aden, Colombo, Fremantle, Melbourne, Sydney
Orsova	February 8	Bermuda, Port Everglades, Nassau, Cristobal, Acapulco, Los Angeles, San Francisco, Vancouver, Honolulu, Suva, Auckland
Himalaya	February 18	Flushing, Gibraltar, Naples, Port Said, Aden, Colombo, Fremantle, Adelaide, Melbourne, Sydney

Another extensive service was the (four) annual around-the-world voyages for Shaw Savill's *Southern Cross* and her running-mate, the *Northern Star*. The former sailed westabout, the latter always eastabout. Twin sailings for 1963 read:

Southern Cross	***Northern Star***
Southampton, May 28	Southampton, August 8
Trinidad, June 6–7	Las Palmas, August 12
Curacao, June 8	Cape Town, August 22–23
Panama, June 10–11	Durban, August 25–26
Tahiti, June 21–22	Fremantle, September 4
Fiji, June 27	Melbourne, September 8–9
Wellington, July 1–3	Sydney, September 11–13
Brisbane, July 7	Wellington, September 16–18
Sydney, July 9–10	Auckland, September 20
Melbourne, July 12–13	Fiji, September 23
Fremantle, July 17	Tahiti, September 27–28
Durban, July 27–28	Panama, October 8–9
Capetown, July 30–31	Curacao, October 11
Las Palmas, August 10	Trinidad, October 12
Southampton, August 14	Barbados, October 13–14
	Southampton, October 22

Until the late '60s, before the worldwide spread of swift jet transport, some British line voyages still offered enormous time at sea. Travel time, while today measured mostly in hours and days, was then determined by weeks and even months. When New Zealand Shipping Company's *Rangitane, Rangitoto* and *Ruahine* left London, there were ten days across the mid-Atlantic to Curacao, then two days to Panama, 12 days to Tahiti and a final eight days to Auckland. The ships then had a six-week wait in New Zealand. A similar pattern was followed by Shaw Savill's quartet of *Athenic, Ceramic, Corinthic* and *Gothic:* 11 days to Curacao, two days to Panama and then 18 days to New Zealand. While P&O–Orient's speedy *Canberra* and *Oriana* made Sydney and Melbourne in just over three weeks, the previous liners on the route such as the *Orcades* and *Himalaya* required four weeks. The aged, pre-war *Strath* class and the *Orontes* took five-six weeks.

At British ports, particularly at London and Liverpool, for important freight and in a time before highly expensive dockside labour and then the efficiency of container shipping, many of the combination passenger-cargo ships had extended stays in home waters. Some ships, like the *Rhodesia Castle* and her two sisters on Union Castle's round-Africa service, might remain along the London Docks for three weeks between arrival and the next outward sailing. Others, such as the Ellerman *City of Port Elizabeth* class, the Blue Funnel combination ships and P&O's *Cathay* and *Chitral*, would arrive at London (or Liverpool), offload their cargo and then sail across to Hamburg, Bremen, Rotterdam and Antwerp before returning to London to load the final cargo and take on passengers. In present-day passenger shipping, cruise-ships rarely remain at any port for more than 24 hours, with 8–12 hours being far more common.

Many of the ships listed here relied heavily on cargo. Outbound from Britain, they often carried general freight—manufactured goods such as automobiles and machinery. Homeward, the manifests reflected the various trades: meats from South America, fruits from the Caribbean, gold and more fruit from South Africa, wool and more refrigerated meat from Australia and New Zealand, and inexpensive manufactured goods from the Far East. Some ships carried only high-grade goods, however. The big Cunard *Queens,* for example, took mail and express items.

Accommodation

The decor of British passenger ships was often created to reflect a homely, familiar comfort: soft chairs, chintzes, veneers, fireplaces, floral prints, warm colours and the ever-present portrait of the Queen. In many ways, these quarters, decorations and tone were unique. As one well-travelled passenger reported, 'You could always tell a British passenger ship by its combined smell of fresh flowers and floor wax'.

The *Queen Elizabeth*'s first class restaurant was one of the ultimate shipboard spaces of its time. It rose three decks in height, sat 850 passengers and was done in Canadian Maple. The floor of the *Queen Mary*'s main lounge was done in Laurel Wood from India. The main deck suites on both *Queens* consisted of a full bedroom, sitting room, trunk room and twin bathrooms. They cost $2,500 per person for a five-day passage in the late '50s. The best suite on the *Windsor Castle* included its own dining area while the *Oriana*'s finest stateroom, known as 'the flat', had its own doorbell. Many passengers, particularly in first class, preferred the same cabin for their annual trips in a favoured ship. Loyalists to the *Andes*, which was often thought to be akin to a club-at-sea, not only asked for the same stateroom with the same attendant steward and stewardess, but for the same table and waiter in the restaurant as well. Aboard Cunard's *Caronia* in the '50s, one elderly woman kept the same steward for several years and then rewarded him with a $100,000 bequest in her last will and testament. On the *Queen Elizabeth 2,* one long-faithful waiter was presented with a brand new Jaguar sports car.

The pre-war splendors of the stately and majestic *Queen Mary* were never quite repeated in later years. Even the *Queen Elizabeth*, which was first fully decorated in 1946, was thought to have less than the same overall grandeur of her earlier running-mate. Nor was the baronial elegance of the *Carnarvon Castle* of 1926 and *Winchester Castle* of 1930 quite duplicated in Union Castle's post-war generation of liners, nor were the highly praised, innovative innards of Orient Line's *Orion* of 1935 equalled by the subsequent *Orcades* of 1948. Beginning in the late '40s especially, there was a steady and increasing trend to use lighter woods, lower ceilings, less imaginative furniture and even fewer pieces of original artwork. Vinyls replaced the carpets and synthetics were used instead of the glossy wood panels.

By contrast has been the trend towards creating creature comforts. While the *Strathaird* and *Strathnaver* of 1931 were the first P&O liners to have running water in all passenger cabins, the same firm's *Royal Princess* of 1984 is the first to have remote control television and mini-refrigerators in all staterooms. While passengers aboard such big liners as the *Canberra* and *Oriana* have at least three swimming pools to choose from, travellers on their way to tropical West Africa in Elder Dempster's *Calabar* and *Winneba* made do with canvas creations placed on deck and filled with seawater.

Of course, accommodation aboard some of the ships listed in these pages was quite austere and basic, far from the nostalgic images of glamour and comfort. On board British India's *Rajula*, third class passengers brought along their own bedding and slept on deck under tarpaulin awnings. Despite their tropic itineraries, and long stays in sweltering ports, air conditioning—even in limited use—was unknown to many of these ships. At best, they had to rely on the early Punkah-Louvre 'forced air' systems. Quarters for the staff were equally inelegant. Aboard Blue Funnel's *Charon* and *Gorgon*, the Chinese stewards slept in sling hammocks and used bucket-style saltwater showers.

The passengers

Millions of passengers have travelled aboard the ships mentioned in these pages. Their voyages have ranged from afternoon crossings on one of the Cunard *Queens*, between Southampton and Cherbourg, to roundtrips to the Caribbean in Fyffes *Camito* or *Golfito*, line voyages to Cape Town on one Union Castle liner, a stay ashore and then homeward on another company liner, to four months around-the-world in one of the P&O liners.

Best remembered and documented of these sailings were, of course, the transatlantic crossings of the famed Cunarders. First class often included film stars, corporate tycoons, government ministers, authors and scientists, and even exiled European royalty. They usually travelled in the best quarters, attended not only by the Cunard staff, but by personal servants as well. Their trunks might be in the storage lockers, a long, black limousine in the hold. Wanting to avoid the openess, the public glare of the first class restaurant, they often used the more secluded, upper deck 'Verandah Grill'. They might be seen occasionally strolling along the boat deck, using one of the Turkish baths or attending a private cocktail party. On the *Queens*, Sir Winston and Lady Churchill attended a variety revue, the Duke and Duchess of Windsor walked the ship's measured mile and Liberace gave a piano recital in the main lounge to benefit the British Seamen's fund. The Queen Mother joined a children's tea party, Fred Astaire danced in the main lounge and Elizabeth Taylor swam in the indoor pool. Photographers and reporters at both ends, at New York and Southampton, swarmed aboard to greet or bid farewell to such celebrated voyagers.

More ordinary travellers enjoyed the comforts of cabin and tourist class, in a style that was best exemplified by Cunard's advertising slogan of the day: 'Getting there is half the fun!' There were films and recitals, dancing and horse-racing, lazy afternoons in deckchairs and spirited games in the squash courts, shopping, massages and exercises, and those classic standards, 'bullion' at eleven and tea at four. Dining was, of course, an event within itself. Among other well advertised details, Cunard claimed to offer no less than six different kinds of bacon for breakfasts aboard the *Queens*.

Life aboard the all-first class cruise-ship *Caronia*, also of Cunard, was just as sumptuous. One wealthy dowager sat at the Captain's table while wearing over £100,000 in jewels, another had fresh flowers delivered to her stateroom every morning of a 90-day world cruise and still others hosted private parties onboard for as many as 200 and 300 of their fellow passengers. At ports of call, more limousines were said to greet the *Caronia* than any other liner.

On the South American run, aboard ships such as Royal Mail's *Amazon* class, there was also an important, although far less publicised and famed, first class. There were the diplomats, wealthy Latin land barons, rich merchants and the prosperous tourists, some of whom made the roundtrip voyage as an escape from bleak British winters. The ships would sail from London and proceed southward to Rio de Janeiro, Santos, Montevideo and Buenos Aires. At the Argentine capital city, all passengers would be sent ashore for several days in a hotel while the ship continued to La Plata to load her all important return cargo, Argentine beef. Once back at Buenos Aires, those roundtrip passengers—along with one-way, northbound traffic—would reboard and begin their homeward journey.

Ships like the *Amazon* also made regular calls at Vigo in Spain and Lisbon in Portugal, where they loaded immigrants into their third class quarters, all bound for resettlement in South America. Homeward, such space was often used by 'reverse' migrants, who were seeking a better life and opportunity in Britain or Europe. There were also budget tourists, students and their teachers, and large families, who well appreciated the inexpensive third class fares.

The passenger routes to Africa were also specialised. Aboard the Union Castle mailships to the Cape, the government and upper business class passengers travelled in first class; tourists, migrants and less important business types went in tourist class. Out to Australia, especially aboard the P&O liners, there were heavy loads of migrants, sailing under a special Australian government fare-assisted programme. The full voyage might cost as little as £10. Occasionally, the tourist class quarters were so well booked that P&O had to use some first class berths. Homeward, although with not quite the same capacity figures, there were those return migrants, those who could not adjust to Australian life, and also those Australians who were returning to Britain or Europe for family visits or touring.

Present day cruise passengers are a very different species from most of the passengers carried on the earlier liners. Most importantly, there is less priority in the destination. Cruise-ships travel to a series of ports, usually in calm, warm weather areas, that are mere diversions to their guests. Usually, passengers rejoin the ship the same day, after several hours of bus excursions. The ships have become well-entertained, well-fed and well-run 'floating hotels,' used for one-and two-week voyages which mostly return to the same port of origin.

Cruising

Britain owned the most illustrious cruise-ship of her time, Cunard's 34,000-ton *Caronia*, commissioned in 1949. She had all of the necessary provisions for total, unrestricted luxury travel: every cabin had private bathroom facilities (a distinction not even shared by first class quarters in the larger *Queens*), there were large sun decks, a permanent outdoor pool, and 600 crewmembers to look after an equal number of long cruise guests (932 was her absolute maximum capacity, but this was only for her very occasional transatlantic 'positioning' crossings).

The *Caronia* followed a prescribed pattern year after year, which began soon after she arrived at New York from Southampton in early January. Her first cruise would be her longest and most diverse, three months or so that either went completely around-the-world, through the Pacific or around Africa. This was followed by a Mediterranean cruise in spring, a North Cape-Scandinavian trip in summer and then another Mediterranean voyage in autumn. She would be back in Britain at the end of the year for annual drydocking and preparation for her next annual cruise programme. The *Caronia*'s schedule from 1962 read:

January 25, 92 days around-the-world: New York, Nassau, Cristobal, Balboa, Acapulco, Los Angeles, Honolulu, Yokohama, Kobe, Hong Kong, Manila, Jesselton, Bali, Singapore, Bangkok, Colombo, Bombay, Aden, Suez, Port Said, Alexandria, Haifa, Naples, Lisbon, New York.

May 1, 39 days Mediterranean: New York, Madeira, Tangier, Palma, Malta, Piraeus, Dubrovnik, Venice, Catania, Messina, Naples, Livorno, Villefranche, Marseilles, Barcelona, Gibraltar, Lisbon, Cherbourg and Southampton (where cruise terminated).

June 28, 45 days North Cape-Scandinavia: New York, Reykjavik, Hammerfest, North Cape, Lyngeseidet, Lofoten Island, Svartisen Glacier, Trondheim, Andalsnes, Hellesylt, Merok, Bergen, Stavanger, Oslo, Stockholm, Helsinki, Visby, Sopot, Copenhagen, Hamburg, Queensferry, Oban, Dun Laoghaire, Glengariff, Le Havre and Southampton (where cruise terminated).

August 31, 31 days Mediterranean: New York, Las Palmas, Tangier, Catania, Messina, Naples, Villefranche, Barcelona, Palma, Malaga, Gibraltar, Lisbon, Ponta Delgada and New York.

October 5, 59 days Mediterranean–Black Sea: New York to Madeira, Casablanca, Tangier, Piraeus, Yalta, Odessa, Constanza, Varna, Istanbul, Port Said, Beirut, Haifa, Dubrovnik, Venice, Catania Messina, Naples, Villefranche, Barcelona, Gibraltar, Lisbon, Cherbourg and Southampton (where cruise terminated).

The *Caronia* had a devoted, club-like following of passengers, some of whom lived aboard for several years at a time. The ports of call became less important (some passengers, in fact, rarely even went ashore) as the ship was a superbly run, completely comfortable and totally secure 'floating resort.' Cunard's finest and usually most senior staff served aboard the *Caronia*.

Another very well known British cruising liner, also with a club-like atmosphere, was Royal Mail's *Andes*. Although built originally, in 1939, for the South American run, she was converted in 1959–60 for year-round cruising. She too had an exceptional service ratio: 500 crew serving 480 passengers. Like the *Caronia*, there were many travellers who looked upon the ship as the 'Club *Andes*' and booked passage in her year after year, sometimes for several voyages at once, and often in the same preferred stateroom and with the same devoted staffmembers to look after them. A strong sense of familiarity, much like revisiting some private hotel, was very important.

Another very popular British cruise-ship was Union Castle's *Reina Del Mar*. Although not intended for the deluxe, high luxury markets of the *Caronia* and *Andes*, this ship's informality and happy mood made her a great favourite with travellers wanting a two or three-week holiday. She too sailed from Southampton, on a varied pattern as her schedule suggests:

***Reina Del Mar* Cruises 1971**

April 1, 15 days to Madeira, Casablanca, Palma, Gibraltar and Lisbon.
April 16, 13 days to Madeira, Teneriffe, Casablanca and Gibraltar.
April 30, 14 days to Lisbon, Palma, Villefranche and Alicante.
May 14th, 12 days to Gibraltar, Casablanca, Teneriffe and Madeira.
May 27, 8 days to Tangier and Lisbon.
June 4, 14 days to Palma, Naples, Gibraltar and Lisbon.
June 19, 18 days to Tangier, Naples, Athens, Malta and Gibraltar.
July 9, 14 days to Azores, Madeira, Teneriffe and Lisbon.
July 23, 14 days to Lisbon, Gibraltar, Naples and Malaga.
August 7, 13 days to Cadiz, Casablanca, Teneriffe and Madeira.
August 20, 14 days to Malaga, Villefranche, Palma and Alicante.
September 4, 13 days to Vigo, Teneriffe, Madeira and Lisbon.
September 17, 14 days to Tangier, Madeira, Las Palmas and Lisbon.
October 2, 20 days to Naples, Athens, Malta, Palma, Tangier and Lisbon.
October 22, 14 days to Madeira, Las Palmas, Casablanca and Gibraltar.

British India's 'schools cruising' was a most unique, highly popular concept. Initially, former troop-ships such as the *Devonia* and *Dunera* were employed, with spaces for some 200 adults and over 800 youngsters. The passenger quarters were quite separate from the student dormitories, and the two groups seemed only to meet during the specialised lectures given during the voyage. Otherwise, almost all forms of entertainment aboard such ships, and most unlike today's highly programmed cruise-ships, was completely improvised, mostly by the passengers and students themselves and the help of one or two ship's officers. One purser aboard the *Dunera* later recounted that his only entertainment equipment was a record player. The educational cruise programme was quite varied and departed from an ever-changing number of British and Mediterranean ports.

Ship	From	To
Nevasa	Southampton	Gibraltar, Tripoli, Istanbul, Piraeus and Venice
Devonia	Tilbury	Lisbon, Malaga, Ceuta and Corunna
Dunera	Genoa	La Goulette, Ibiza, Cadiz and Lisbon
Nevasa	Venice	Piraeus, Istanbul, Malta and Gibraltar
Devonia	Tilbury	Vigo, Malaga, Tangier and Lisbon
Dunera	Invergordon	Amsterdam, Copenhagen and Bergen
Devonia	London	Bergen, Oslo and Gothenburg
Nevasa	Le Havre	Cape Breton Island and Montreal
Dunera	Grangemouth	Gothenburg, Riga and Kristiansand
Devonia	Tilbury	Vigo, Lisbon and Brest
Dunera	Grangemouth	Bergen, Copenhagen and Amsterdam
Devonia	Avonmouth	Olden, Bergen and Copenhagen
Nevasa	Southampton	Teneriffe, Ceuta and Vigo
Nevasa	Swansea	Madeira, Casablanca, Gibraltar and Lisbon
Dunera	Greenock	Vigo, Tangier, Lisbon and Zeebrugge

Unfortunately, by the early '80s, much of the student trade for the *Uganda*, the last remaining British India educational cruise-ship, had fallen away. Hard hit by worldwide inflation, youngsters could no longer independently raise the fares for a two-week voyage. While the adult trade remained strong and loyal, the comparatively low numbers (306 berths on the *Uganda*) could not sustain the operation of such an ageing ship. Called to duty as a hospital ship during the Falklands campaign of 1982, the *Uganda* was then recalled soon afterward for use as relay ship between Ascension and the Falklands. Having a very lucrative, secure charter for this veteran liner, P&O—as the parent of British India—ended educational cruises completely. Many passengers still mourn the loss.

In the early '70s, as the last of their traditional overseas liner operations declined considerably, P&O sold off most of their older ships, such as *Orcades, Himalaya* and *Orsova*, and were restyled as P&O Cruises. Accurately, they saw this as their future in passenger shipping. The giant *Canberra* and *Oriana* were made one-class, each with over 1,700 berths, and sent on two and three-week cruise voyages from Southampton. For the Australian market, the Company retained the *Arcadia*, dating from 1954, which cruised out of Sydney to the South Pacific and Far East, and which was later replaced by the former Swedish *Kungsholm*, refitted as the *Sea Princess*.

Life aboard the present-day *Canberra* is very different from her earlier years, as a two-class ship on the Australian run. Then, there was very little 'planned' entertainment; passengers created their own diversions, from talent shows to fancy dress. Presently, the daily programmes are far more extended:

8.00 am	Radio Canberra
10.00 am	Keep fit class
10.00 am	Children's cinema
10.30 am	Meet the hostess
11.00 am	Stroll a mile
11.00 am	Deck games
11.00 am	Flower Lecture
11.00 am	Jackpot Bingo
11.30 am	Morning Singalong
Noon	Mid-day Melodies in the Bar
Noon	Noontime announcements
2.30 pm	Cards & Games
2.45 pm	Whist Drive
2.45 pm	Deck Competition Finals
2.45 pm	Recipe Swap
2.45 pm	Golf Tuition
2.45 pm	Teenage Circuit Training
2.45 pm	Feature film in the cinema
3.30 pm	White Elephant Sale
4.30 pm	Jackpot Bingo
5.00 pm	Dance Class
5.00 pm	Teenage Cricket Match
5.00 pm	Children's disco
5.30 pm	Individual Quiz
6.00 pm	Radio Canberra
6.30 pm	Hoy
6.30 pm	Pre-dinner Cocktail Music
7.45 pm	Pre-dinner Cocktail Music
8.15 pm	Early Evening Cards & Games
8.15 pm	Early Evening Dancing
8.30 pm	Individual Quiz
8.30 pm	Farewell Variety Show, 1st sitting
8.30 pm	Bingo
8.30 pm	Early Evening Whist Drive
9.30 pm	Early Evening Disco
9.30 pm	Carry On Dancing
9.30 pm	Joker 7 & Blackjack
9.45 pm	Late Night Whist Drive
9.45 pm	Bingo
9.45 pm	Feature film in the cinema
10.00 pm	Farewell Variety Show, 2nd sitting
11.00 pm	Disco 81
11.30 pm	Orchestra Dancing
11.30 pm	Joker 7 & Blackjack
Midnight	Auld Lang Syne

***Canberra*, Thursday, September 10, 1981**

Aircraft, which earlier displaced so many ships listed in these ships, are today a friendly cohort. Many cruise voyages, such as those aboard P&O's *Sea Princess*, are a combination of air-sea planning. Passengers might fly out to Athens, connect with the ship and then spend two weeks cruising to Istanbul, Yalta, Constanta, Dikili, Corfu, Trieste and Venice (and then the connecting flight homeward to London). These flights are usually scheduled for same-day links to and from the ship. It's all very convenient and uncomplicated; passengers purchase one set of tickets that include the flights, shipboard accommodation and even the shoreside transfers.

On longer cruises, say 90 days around-the-world on the *Queen Elizabeth 2*, *Canberra* and *Sea Princess*, segments of these voyages have become very popular offerings. Passengers can take, for example, only the first three weeks of a journey, say from Southampton to San Francisco via the Caribbean, Florida, Panama and Mexico, and then disembark and return to Britain by air. Alternately, they can fly out to San Francisco, join the ship and sail out to Honolulu, Fiji and Sydney, and then return home, again by air. As cruise companies seek to expand their markets and introduce cruise travel to a new generation of travellers, more and more voyage possibilities (and time frames) aboard well-entertained, well-provisioned ships must be offered. As one cruise line suggested, 'In today's highly competitive passenger ship business, we must offer something for everyone—from a few days to a few months.

The American cruise trade is the busiest and most highly specialised in the world, and employs over 60 ships. Firms such as Cunard have the major share of their fleet in this trade: the *Queen Elizabeth 2* cruises from not only New York, but Boston, Philadelphia, Norfolk, Port Everglades and Los Angeles too; the *Cunard Countess* in the Caribbean from San Juan; the *Cunard Princess* on the West Coast, summers to Alaska from Vancouver and the remaining time to Mexico from Los Angeles. The recently acquired *Sagafjord* and *Vistafjord* also operate on a seasonally diverse pattern of sailings. Even the *QE2*'s part-time transatlantic crossings, the last of their kind out of New York and Southampton, are largely supported by American travellers and run more like cruise voyages. Much of Cunard's passenger ship management is now, in fact, based at New York.

In order to keep pace with the rapidly changing American cruise industry, even the *QE2* has had to undergo periodic refits, modernisations and upgradings. More suites, including two very deluxe penthouses, had to be added. Additional shops were placed aboard, the gambling and casino facilities expanded and even a passenger computer centre added. The restaurants have been altered and reworked, and the catering system revised. One of the aft-deck outdoor pools has now been covered by a retractable, weather-resistant sliding glass dome and adjoins yet another addition, a full health spa. In addition, a constant programme of almost never ending passenger entertainment and diversion, similar to the aforementioned daily outline for the *Canberra*, is essential. However, there are some additions, such as a regular list of guest lecturers, used for mid-morning and afternoon talk sessions. On a recent five-day Atlantic crossing, there was a film star, a noted mystery author, a celebrated decorator and the head of British Airways' Concorde fleet. On the longer, more expensive cruises, such as the three-month trip around-the-world, entertainments, instructors and lecturers aboard the *QE2* are changed at regular intervals.

In January 1985, the *QE2* left New York on a 95-day circumnavigation that included calls at Port Everglades, Port-au-Prince, Cartagena, Cristobal, Balboa, Acapulco, Los Angeles, Papeete, Moorea, Rarotonga, Auckland, Wellington, Christchurch, Sydney, Hobart, Adelaide, Perth, Bali, Manila, Hong Kong, Pattaya, Singapore, Kelang, Colombo, Bombay, the Seychelles, Durban, Cape Town, Santos, Rio de Janeiro, Salvador, Martinique, St Thomas and Port Everglades. Fares ranged from £21,000 to over £200,000 in one of the top-deck penthouses. With her capacity especially reduced to 1,200, about one-third of the passengers made the entire journey; the remaining 800 or so beds were used by steadily changing guests, who took two and three-week portions of the trip. On one of the earlier cruises, an Asian sultan came aboard for a week's passage to Hong Kong with his party of 25!

Wanting to rapidly expand into the cruise business, especially in America, P&O bought the Seattle-based Princess Cruises in the mid-'70s. They had an immediate fleet of three modern ships, the *Island Princess, Pacific Princess* and *Sun Princess*. Based mostly along the West Coast, at Los Angeles and San Francisco, sailings are offered to Alaska (in summer), Mexico, the Caribbean and even several long-distance runs to the South Pacific and Australia.

Presently, Princess is one of the dominant firms in the US cruise trade. While their ships offer substantial entertainment programmes, all quite similar to the *QE2* and *Canberra*, they have also been noted for creating popular 'theme' and 'special interest' cruises, voyages that include a series of lectures and programmes linked to a specialty topic. This is yet another marketing technique in a highly competitive business. There have been 'Hollywood Nostalgia' cruises, with long-ago film stars and their films aboard; 'wine tasting' cruises and others on gardening, the stock market and investing, beauty and fitness, astronomy, astrology, classical music, country and western dancing and even 'computer' cruises. Cunard's *QE2* occasionally follows this trend and, in January 1985, offered the first 'trivial pursuit' cruise, which was based on a highly popular game of trivial knowledge.

In the early '80s, as the American cruise trade grew to a $4 billion level, several major firms invested in new, larger ships. Princess ordered their biggest liner yet from the Wartsila Shipyards in Finland. Costing some $160 million, making her the most expensive British passenger ship ever, she was named *Royal Princess* by the Princess of Wales while berthed at Southampton in

November 1984. Housed in a futuristic profile, this liner—which can carry over 1,200 passengers—has been called 'the first cruise-ship for the 21st century'. Every cabin, for example, has its own remote control television, a mini-refrigerator and many even have a private verandah.

The British cruise market has not grown as buoyantly, especially in recent years. There is less of a seagoing leisure market and considerable competition from those highly popular 'flights to the sun,' which go to Mediterranean and North African destinations often at bargain rates. The *Canberra* and *Sea Princess* of P&O are the last full-time Southampton-based cruise-ships. Other, more occasional cruise sailings are offered by the *QE2* and several foreign-flag liners.

While the general British passenger ship fleet has been reduced greatly over the past quarter century, the remaining liners—such as the *QE2, Canberra* and new *Royal Princess*—are proud successors to the likes of the earlier *Queen Mary, Stratheden* and *Andes*. Long may they sail!

Withdrawal and decline

The gradual and then the very swift decline of this last big British passenger fleet began in the early '60s. Ironically, it started with the most distinguished and luxurious trade of all, the North Atlantic. Soon after the first commercial jetliner crossed to London in the autumn of 1958, the airlines began their devastating, merciless intrusion into trans-atlantic travel. Six days to Britain became six hours. In a matter of months, the jets had secured almost two-thirds of the total traffic: 1.5 million by air against nearly 882,000 by sea.

The Cunard Company, which had the largest Atlantic liner fleet and which carried a third of all passengers who made crossings in the mid-'50s, were at first most reluctant to admit (or at least recognise) the potential challenge of the jets. From their wood-panelled boardroom at Liverpool, they felt that there would always be a place for transatlantic liners, that a steady and loyal clientel would always prefer the likes of the *Queen Mary* and *Queen Elizabeth*. However, within three years, by 1961, the two giant *Queens* began to slip deeply into the red.

The inevitable drop in Atlantic liner passengers and the gradual shift to more lucrative cruising was difficult to ignore by this time. First, they had to cancel plans for a projected 27,000-tonner, to replace the 30-year-old *Britannic*, the last of the original White Star liners. Soon afterward, two of the relatively new Canadian ships, the *Saxonia* and *Ivernia*, were sent to their builder's yard for major improvements and transformations to become the competitive winter cruise-ships *Carmania* and *Franconia*. Next, the venerable *Mauretania*, a longtime favourite on the Atlantic run to New York, was repainted in Cunard's 'cruising green' and restyled for more one-class leisure trips. She even had a misplaced season sailing out of the Mediterranean, an area where the company could hardly be expected to have a respectable share of the market.

It was all becoming rather desperate. Even the unsuited *Queens* were sent on periodic trips to the tropics, from New York to the Bahamas and from Southampton to the Canaries. However, since these ageing ships lacked the necessary lido decks, outdoor pools and had, at best, limited air-conditioning systems, they appealed mostly to a curious, nostalgic audience. The *Queens* were each losing £750,000 annually by 1966.

A year later, in 1967, the Cunard management faced the harsh, but honest reality: Almost the entire passenger fleet was outmoded, uncompetitive in the growing cruise trades, and would have to be retired. In a period of some 15 months, beginning that September, the company decommissioned the *Queen Mary, Queen Elizabeth, Caronia, Carinthia* and *Sylvania*. All that was left was the renovated *Carmania* and *Franconia*, and then the new superliner *Queen Elizabeth 2*, which was delivered in early 1969. A few years later, in 1972, even those two older ships were finished-off, being replaced by a brand new, supposedly more economical team named *Cunard Adventurer* and *Cunard Ambassador*. By the early '70s, Cunard was wanting to rid itself of its earlier, more formal image and even the traditional 'ia' names disappeared.

Canadian Pacific faced similar problems on the Atlantic. Soon after introducing the *Empress of Canada* in 1961, they had to face some serious decision-making. The earlier sister-ships *Empress of Britain* and *Empress of England* were detoured to undertake more cruising, not only from Liverpool and Southampton, but from Cape Town as well, and often while under charter to the innovative Travel Savings Association. This latter firm, while short-lived, offered inexpensive

Also originally designed as a four-master, the Derbyshire *was refitted after the Second World War with a more eye-pleasing profile of twin masts and a single wide funnel* (Alex Duncan).

Derbyshire

Service Liverpool to Rangoon via Suez (same as *Worcestershire*). **Particulars** 10,641 gross tons; 501 × 66 × 29 ft. **Builder** Fairfield Shipbuilding & Engineering Company, Glasgow, Scotland, 1935. **Machinery** Sulzer diesels, twin screw. Speed 14½ knots. **Capacity** 115 first class. **Notes** Originally four-masted design. Original capacity 291 first class. 1939–42 sailed as Armed Merchant Cruiser, then until 1946 as a troop-ship. Rebuilt 1946–48. Arrived at Hong Kong for scrapping in February 1964.

Devonshire

Service Government trooping only—Mediterranean, Middle East, Africa, etc. **Particulars** 12,773 gross tons; 517 × 63 × 24 ft. **Builders** Fairfield Shipbuilding & Engineering Company, Glasgow, Scotland, 1939. Sulzer diesels, twin screw. Speed 13½ knots. **Capacity** 130 first class, 96 second class, 99 third class, 824 troops. **Notes** Sister-ship to British India's *Dunera*. 1939–46 wartime service. Major refit 1953–54. Sold January 1962 to British India Line to become educational cruise-ship *Devonia (qv)*.

Warwickshire and *Leicestershire*

Service Liverpool to Port Said, Port Sudan, Aden, Colombo and Rangoon. **Particulars** 8,917/8,922 gross tons respectively; 498 × 60 × 27 ft. **Builders** Fairfield Shipbuilding Engineering Company, Glasgow, 1948 and 1949 respectively. **Machinery** Steam turbines, single screw. Speed 14½ knots. **Capacity** 76 first class. **Notes** Sister-ships. *Warwickshire* reduced to 12-passenger freighter in 1964, then sold to Typaldos Lines of Greece and re-named *Hania*. 1965–66 rebuilt as Mediterranean ferry: 1,450 passengers, 100 autos, 80 coaches. Tonnage increased to 11,300. Briefly listed as

DEVONSHIRE

Above left *The* Devonshire *was built especially as a peacetime trooper* (B. Reeves).
Below left *The* Warwickshire *earned income not only from her 76 passengers but also from her five cargo holds* (J. K. Byass).
Above *Commissioned in 1957, Bibby's* Oxfordshire *proved to be Britain's last peacetime trooper. She was withdrawn in 1962 and thereafter all service personnel were airlifted to their destinations* (Roger Sherlock).

world's largest ferry. Laid-up 1967 following collapse of Typaldos. 1971 sold to K Lines, Greece. 1972 sold to Hellenic Cruises and re-named *Sirius*. Never used. Scrapped 1980 at Skaramanga, Greece. *Leicestershire* chartered to British India 1950–54 for East African service. Made final Bibby passenger sailing in 1964. Sold a year later to Typaldos Lines. Refitted as Aegean ferry *Heraklion*. Sank during Aegean storm on December 8 1966. Lost within 15 minutes with 241 casualties. Eventually found to be unsafely loaded and prompted collapse of Typaldos.

Oxfordshire

Service Government trooping—Mediterranean, Far East, Africa, etc. **Particulars** 20,586 gross tons; 609 × 78 × 26 ft. **Builder** Fairfield Shipbuilding & Engineering Company, Glasgow, Scotland, 1957. **Machinery** Steam turbines, twin screw. Speed 17 knots. **Capacity** 220 first class, 100 second class, 180 third class, 1,000 troops. **Notes** 1957–62 sailed as Britain's last full-time troop-ship. Sold in 1962 to Sitmar Line, Liberian flag and rebuilt in Holland for Australian service as *Fairstar*. 1,910 berths fitted. Began cruise service only in 1973 from Australian ports. Still in service.

Blue Funnel Line

The Blue Funnel Line was formed in 1866, but in fact did not enter the passenger trades until 1910. The company, although best known under its rather distinctive name, prompted by an early ship with a funnel painted in a vivid blue, was actually part of Alfred Holt & Company, a mighty Liverpool-based organisation that later owned the China Mutual Steam Navigation Company and Ocean Steam Ship Company.

LONDON

Blue Funnel's earliest shipping interests were in the China tea trades, using coal burners that took nine weeks for the passage between London and Shanghai. Passenger services opened only after the firm extended its trading to Australia soon after the turn of the century.

The business eventually prospered to include even local, short-sea services out of Singapore, a port often thought to be Blue Funnel's second home. After World War 2, a new policy called for only limited passenger spaces in high standard combination ships. These survived until the mid-'60s, when these final ships were downgraded to 12-passenger freighter class. Blue Funnel's final passenger ship, the *Centaur* of 1963, was transferred to Singapore registry in 1973.

Gorgon and *Charon*

Service Singapore to Fremantle. **Particulars** 3,678/3,964 gross tons respectively; 336 × 51 × 20 ft. **Builder** Caledon Shipbuilding & Engineering Company, Dundee, Scotland, 1933/1936 respectively. **Machinery** Burmeister & Wain diesel, single screw. Speed 13½ knots. **Capacity** 72/88 one-class. **Notes** Near sister-ships. Both scrapped 1964, *Gorgon* at Hong Kong and *Charon* at Singapore. *Charon* briefly re-named *Seng Kong No. 1* prior to scrapping.

Gunung Djati

Service Pilgrim service in Indian Ocean, mostly between Indonesia and Jeddah. **Particulars** 17,891 gross tons; 577 × 72 × 25 ft. **Builder** Blohm & Voss Shipbuilders, Hamburg, Germany, 1936. **Machinery** Steam turbines, twin screw. Speed 16 knots. **Capacity** 106 first class, over 2,000 pilgrims. **Notes** Built as *Pretoria* for German-East Africa Line. 1939–45 used as Nazi accommodation then hospital ship. Seized by British invasion forces in May 1945; re-named as *Empire Doon* for British government trooping. Major refit 1948–49; re-named *Empire Orwell* for further trooping. Chartered to Pan Islamic Steamship Company of Karachi for pilgrim service in 1958. Same year sold outright to Blue Funnel for conversion to pilgrim ship. Resumed service March 1959 as *Gunung Djati*. Sold to the Indonesian Government in 1962; later listed to Pelni Line, then Arafat Line. Major refit and converted to motorship at Hong Kong in 1973. Survived shipyard fire as well. Re-classified as a military troop-ship and accommodation centre in 1977 and re-named *Kri Tanjung Pandan*. Still in service at Jakarta in 1985.

Peleus and *Pyrrhus*

Service Liverpool, Rotterdam, Port Said, Singapore, Manila, Hong Kong, Kobe and Yokohama. **Particulars** 10,093 gross tons; 516 × 68 × 30 ft. **Builder** Cammell Laird & Company Limited, Birkenhead, England, 1949. **Machinery** Steam turbines, single screw. Speed 18½ knots. **Capacity** 30 first class. **Notes** 'P' Class sister-ships—*Peleus, Pyrrhus, Patroclus* and *Perseus*. *Peleus* reduced to 12-passenger freighter in 1967. Scrapped at Kaohsiung, Taiwan 1972. *Pyrrhus* seriously damaged by fire at Liverpool Docks on November 12 1964. Rebuilt as a freighter. Scrapped at Kaohsiung, Taiwan in 1972.

Patroclus and *Perseus*

Service Liverpool, Rotterdam, Port Said, Singapore, Manila, Hong Kong, Kobe and Yokohama. **Particulars** 10,109 gross tons; 516 × 68 × 30 ft. **Builder** Vickers-Armstrong Shipbuilders Limited, Newcastle, England, 1950. **Machinery** Steam turbines, single screw. Speed 18½ knots. **Capacity** 30 first class. **Notes** Sister-ships to *Peleus* and *Pyrrhus*. *Patroclus* reduced to 12-passenger freighter in 1967. Transferred to China Mutual Steam Navigation Company, British flag, in 1972 and re-named *Philoctetes*. Scrapped 1973 at Kaohsiung, Taiwan. *Perseus* reduced to freighter in 1967. Scrapped at Kaohsiung in 1973.

Helenus, Jason, Hector and *Ixion*

Service Liverpool, Port Said, Aden, Albany or Fremantle, Adelaide, Melbourne and Sydney. **Parti-**

Above left *Blue Funnel's* Charon *and her near-sister, the* Gorgon, *traded in distant waters—between Singapore and Australia* (World Ship Society Photo Library).
Left *Built originally in 1936, as Germany's* Pretoria, *this former liner sailed for some years as the British troopship* Empire Orwell. *Shown at the Southampton Docks, she later became the pilgrim ship* Gunung Djati (Michael Cassar).

Above *Blue Funnel's* Pyrrhus *and her sister-ships were typical passenger-cargo liners of the post-war era. They carried 30 passengers in high standard accommodation as well as six holds of cargo* (Michael Cassar).
Below *The Blue Funnel ships were almost always recognisable—both by their distinctive blue stack colouring and their Greek mythological names. However ships such as the* Perseus *became increasingly unprofitable by the late 1960s as airlines took their passenger trade and larger container ships secured the bulk of the cargo business* (Alex Duncan).
Above right *Blue Funnel's* Helenus *at Valletta, Malta with the Tirrenia Line's* Citta Di Tunisi *moored just behind* (Michael Cassar).
Below right *The classically beautiful* Jason *sailing from Cape Town* (Alex Duncan).

JASON

Above *The engines – aft* Centaur *of 1963 was the last Blue Funnel Line passenger ship* (C. B. Mulholland).
Above right *Blue Star's quartet of combination passenger-cargo liners included the* Uruguay Star *wearing the black hull colouring which remained until 1959* (Alex Duncan).
Below right *The* Brasil Star *in the dove-grey hull colour* (Alex Duncan).

culars 10,129/10,160/10,125/10,125 gross tons respectively; 523 × 69 × 31 ft. **Builders** Harland & Wolff Limited, Belfast, Northern Ireland (*Jason* by Swan, Hunter & Wigham Richardson Limited, Newcastle-upon-Tyne, England), 1949–50. **Machinery** Steam turbines, single screw. Speed 18½ knots. **Capacity** 30 first class. **Notes** Four sister-ships. All reduced to freighters in 1964, then scrapped at Kaohsiung, Taiwan in 1972.

Centaur
Service Singapore to Fremantle. **Particulars** 8,262 gross tons; 480 × 66 × 22 feet. **Builder** John Brown & Company Limited, Clydebank, Scotland, 1963. **Machinery** Burmeister & Wain diesels, twin screw. Speed 20 knots. **Capacity** 190 first class. **Notes** Entered service January 1964. Last Blue Funnel passenger ship. Sailings restyled in 1978 to occasionally include Hong Kong and Manila. Given Singapore registry in 1973 and re-registered to China Mutual Steam Navigation Company Limited and then to Straits Steamship Company. Chartered to Curnow Shipping Company for Avonmouth–St Helena–South Africa service from November 1982 until January 1984. Sold spring 1985 to Chinese to become the *Hai Long* for China coastal service.

Blue Star Line
The Blue Star Line started soon after the turn of the century with very concentrated efforts on the meat trade from South America, particularly from the Argentine. Other freighter runs were eventually established to the North American Pacific Coast and to

URUGUAY STAR

BRASIL STAR

Australia and New Zealand. Passenger sailings began in 1927, but only on the South American run. One of these early ships, the *Arandora Star*, was later converted for deluxe cruising in the '30s and established a reputation that is remembered to this day. In the post-war rebuilding scheme, only four new combination sister-ships, with a space for some 50 passengers, were commissioned. They survived until the early '70s. Thereafter their highly perishable cargo went in new, high speed freighters and then in the advanced generation of container-ships. Present-day Blue Star passenger operations (1984) are limited to a pair of container-ships carrying two passengers each on a run from the American West Coast to the South Pacific.

Argentina Star, Brasil Star, Uruguay Star and *Paraguay Star*

Service London to Lisbon, Madeira, Las Palmas, Teneriffe, Recife, Salvador, Rio de Janeiro, Santos, Montevideo and Buenos Aires. **Particulars** 10,716/10,716/10,722/10,723 gross tons; 503 × 68 × 31 ft. **Builder** Cammell Laird & Company, Birkenhead, England, 1947–48. **Machinery** Steam turbines, single screw. Speed 16 knots. **Capacity** 51/53/53/53 first class. **Notes** Four sister-ships. Final Blue Star passenger ships. All were repainted with grey hull colouring in 1959. *Paraguay Star* seriously damaged by fire at London on August 12 1969. Beyond economic repair; scrapped at Hamburg. Three others scrapped at Kaohsiung, Taiwan in 1972.

Iberia Star

Service London to Lisbon, Las Palmas, Rio de Janeiro, Santos, Montevideo and Buenos Aires. **Particulars** 10,854 gross tons; 505 × 65 × 27 ft. **Builder** John Cockerill S/A, Hoboken, Belgium, 1950. **Machinery** Burmeister & Wain diesel, single screw. Speed 16 knots. **Capacity** 76 first class. **Notes** 1950–61 sailed for the Belgian Line first as *Baudouinville*, then *Thysville*. Antwerp–Congo service. 217 passengers. 1961 sold to Booth Line, British flag; re-named *Anselm (qv)*. Amazon service. Sold to Blue Star in 1963 and rebuilt at

The former Belgian liner Thysville *had been sold to the Booth Line in 1961 becoming the* Anselm *for the Amazon trade. In 1963 she was rebuilt for Blue Star as the* Iberia Star (Roger Sherlock).

Bremen with altered passenger and refrigerator cargo space. Entered Blue Star service August 1964. Transferred to Austasia Line of Singapore in 1965 for Singapore–Australia service. Re-named *Australasia.* 1971–72 plagued with mechanical problems. Scrapped at Hualien, Taiwan in July 1973.

Booth Line

The Booth Line began trading to the remote Amazon Delta in 1866, using two very small steamers. The company was then little more than a family business. However, the uniqueness of the Amazon region soon showed great fortune. As the trade expanded and other foreign flag firms arrived, Booth retained dominance, a position held for decades to come. Bought out finally in 1946 by Blue Star, Booth retained itse separate identity. The passenger division was discontinued in the mid-'60s and was replaced by small freighters, most of which were later transferred to overseas 'flags of convenience.' Booth no longer trades as a British shipping firm.

Hubert

Service Liverpool to Leixoes, Lisbon, Madeira, Barbados, Trinidad, Belem and Manaus. **Particulars** 8,062 gross tons; 439 × 60 × 25 ft. **Builder** Cammell Laird & Company, Birkenhead, England, 1955. **Machinery** Steam turbines, single screw. Speed 15 knots. **Capacity** 74 first class, 96 tourist class. **Notes** Maiden voyage February 1955. Withdrawn from Booth Line service October 1964. Company's final passenger ship. Sold to Austasia Line of Singapore in 1965 for Singapore–Australia service. Re-named *Malaysia.* Aground at Djakarta May 1971. Withdrawn May 1976 and sold to Middle Eastern Express Lines; rebuilt as a livestock carrier. Re-named *Khaleej Express* for Australia–Middle East sheep run. Transferred to Saudi Arabian flag. Scrapped 1984 at Karachi.

Anselm

Service Liverpool to the Amazon (same as *Hubert*). **Particulars** 10,950 gross tons; 505 × 65 × 27 ft. **Builder** John Cockerill S/A, Hoboken, Belgium, 1950. **Machinery** Burmeister & Wain diesel, single screw.

Booth Line's former Hubert *went on to become the Singapore-based* Malaysia, *sailing with passengers and general cargo to Australian ports. Her third and last life was as a Saudi Arabian sheep carrier* (Michael Cassar).

Speed 16 knots. **Capacity** 128 first class, 100 tourist class. **Notes** 1950–61 sailed for the Belgian Line as *Baudouninville*, then as *Thysville* on Antwerp—Congo run. 217 passengers. Sold to Booth Line, British flag in 1961; re-named *Anselm*. 1963 sold to Blue Star Line and re-named *Iberia Star (qv)*.

British India Steam Navigation Company Ltd

The British India Steam Navigation Company Limited ranks among the world's greatest and most historic shipping firms. When created in 1862, its primary purpose was to provide an extensive network of Indian Ocean as well as localised, short-sea services from both Bombay and Calcutta. It was the maritime reflection of the erstwhile Indian Empre, which was soon to become part of the British Empire. Services, including passenger runs, were later expanded to include East and South Africa, Australia and even along the Far East. The company's close trading relationship with the larger P&O Company resulted finally in a merger, created in 1914, but which allowed for separate corporate identities. P&O was the more dominant partner, however, having 12 of the combined 20 board directors while British India was limited to eight.

Almost all of the original 'BI' passenger services were ended by the early '70s—victim of either aircraft competition, increased operational costs and/or newly formed nationalised shipping rivals. The *Dwarka* terminated the last of the Bombay passenger sailings in 1982. British India's educational cruising programme, begun in the '30s with unemployed troop-ships, was re-started in the '60s and continued until 1983, when the last of these specialised cruise-ships, the *Uganda,* was withdrawn from commercial service. Having worked out her charter to the British government for service in the South Atlantic the *Uganda* is now (autumn 1985) laid up in the River Fal awaiting disposal.

Below *The* Anselm *had a brief two-year stint on the Amazon trade for the Booth Line* (Alex Duncan).
Above right *Three British India liners together at Mombasa in 1963: the* Uganda *is on the left, the* Karanja *at anchor and the* Kenya *on the right* (P&O Group).
Below right *Three East African liners at Kilindini in Kenya in 1962: the* Uganda *is at the far left, Lloyd Triestino's* Europa *in centre position and the* Kenya *on the right* (P&O Group).

Rajula

Service Between Madras, Nagapattinam, Penang and Singapore. **Particulars** 8,496 gross tons; 477 × 62 × 26 ft. **Builder** Barclay Curle & Company Limited, Glasgow, Scotland, 1926. **Machinery** Steam triple expansion engines, twin screw. Speed 12 knots. **Capacity** 37 first class, 133 second class, 1,600 deck class. **Notes** 49-year career. 1926–39 passenger capacity listed as over 5,000, the largest ever for a deep-sea passenger ship. 1939–46 War service as troop-ship, then ambulance transport. 1973 retired from British India service; sold to Shipping Corporation of India, Indian flag, and re-named *Rangat*. Government service only. Mechanically exhausted by 1975; scrapped at Bombay.

Dunera

Service Government trooping—Mediterranean, Middle and Far East, etc. From 1961 onwards used for educational cruising, mostly from British ports. **Particulars** 12,615 gross tons; 517 × 63 × 25 ft. **Builder** Barclay Curle & Company Limited, Glasgow, Scotland, 1937. **Machinery** Doxford diesels, twin screw. Speed 14 knots. **Capacity** 123 first class, 95 second class, 100 third class, 831 troops. **Notes** First commercial ship designed purposely to transport government troops. Sister-ship to Bibby Line's *Devonshire*. Entered service August 1937. 1939–45 War service. Major refit 1951. Ended troop service in 1960; refitted for educational cruising. Accommodation re-styled for 188 adults and 834 students. 1967 sold to Spanish shipbreakers and scrapped at Bilbao.

Devonia

Service Educational cruising mostly from British ports to the Mediterranean, Northern Europe, Scandinavia, etc. 2–3 week voyages. **Particulars** 12,796 gross tons; 517 × 63 × 24 ft. **Builder** Fairfield Shipbuilding & Engineering Company, Glasgow, Scotland, 1939. **Machinery** Sulzer diesels, twin screw. Speed 13 knots. **Capacity** 194 adults, 834 students. **Notes** Sister-ship to *Dunera*. 1939–61 sailed as *Devonshire* for Bibby Line *(qv)*. Bought by British India in 1962 and refitted at Glasgow for educational cruising. Re-named *Devonia*. Sold to Italian breakers in late 1967 and scrapped at La Spezia.

Below left *British India's* Rajula *had a career that spanned 49 years* (Roger Sherlock).
British India had tremendous success with its school cruising programme. The two oldest passenger ships on this run were the Dunera **above** *and her near-sister, the* Devonia **below,** *the former* Devonshire *of the Bibby Line* (Michael D. J. Lennon and Alex Duncan).

Above *Like almost all of the British India liners the* Aronda *was painted with a black hull until the mid 1950s and then was changed to a more tropical white* (P&O Group).
Above right *The* Dumra *and her three sister-ships were distinctly built for the Bombay—Persian Gulf trade* (World Ship Society Photo Library).
Below right *The ill-fated* Dara *on fire following a bomb explosion on April 8 1961* (P&O Group).

Amra

Service Bombay (with occasional calls at Porebunder, Bedibunder and Karachi) to Mombasa and Dar-es-Salaam. **Particulars** 8,314 gross tons; 461 × 61 × 23 ft. **Builder** Swan, Hunter & Wigham Richardson Limited, Newcastle-upon-Tyne, England, 1938. **Machinery** Steam turbines, twin screw. Speed 16 knots. **Capacity** 222 saloon class, 737 third class. **Notes** Sister-ship to *Aronda*. Used as wartime hospital ship 1939–45. Scrapped in the Far East in 1966.

Aronda

Service Karachi to Colombo and Chittagong. **Particulars** 8,396 gross tons; 461 × 61 × 23 ft. **Builder** Swan, Hunter & Wigham Richardson Limited, Newcastle-upon-Tyne, England, 1941. **Machinery** Steam turbines, twin screw. Speed $16\frac{1}{2}$ knots. **Capacity** 44 first class, 22 second class, 28 interchangeable, 60 intermediate, 1,800 deck class. **Notes** Sister-ship to *Amra*. War service 1941–45. Sailed for British India until 1963. Broke away from tug *Cabrilla* while under tow on July 21 1963, bound for Kaohsiung scrapyards. *Aronda* went aground on the Chinese coast, southwest of Macao. Finally refloated by Chinese authorities in December 1963; proceeded to Kaohsiung and scrapped.

Dumra and *Dara*

Service Bombay and Karachi to Persian Gulf ports: Pasni, Gnadur, Muscat, Bandar Abbas, Shahjab, Dubai, Umm Said, Bahrain, Bushire, Kuwait, Abadan, Khorramshahr and Basrah. **Particulars** 4,867/5,030 gross tons; 399 × 55 × 22 ft. **Builder** Barclay Curle & Company Limited, Glasgow, Scotland, 1946 and 1948. **Machinery** Doxford diesel, single screw. Speed 14 knots. **Capacity** 13/13 first class, 41/65 second class, 1,100/950 deck class. **Notes** Part of 'D' Class sister-ships: *Dumra* (1946), *Dwarka* (1947), *Dara* (1948) and *Daressa* (1950). *Dumra* laid-up May 1978. Sold in February 1979 to local scrappers at Bombay.

Dara destroyed by terrorist bomb explosion and subsequent fire while on a passage from Basrah to Bombay on April 8 1961. Exact casualties uncertain but believed to be approximately 200. After being abandoned by crew and passengers and under tow of tug *Ocean Salvor*, she sank on April 10.

Above *The* Daressa *in her original black hull colouring as built* (P&O Group).
Below *The* Sirdhana *at Hong Kong in the earlier black British India livery. Note the Chinese characters along her hull just below the superstructure* (P&O Group).
Above right *The* Sirdhana *as she appeared in later years with the white hull* (P&O Group).

Dwarka and *Daressa*

Service Bombay and Karachi to Persian Gulf ports (same as for *Dumra*). **Particulars** 4,851/4,180 gross tons; 399 × 55 × 22 ft. **Builder** Swan, Hunter & Wigham Richardson Limited, Newcastle-upon-Tyne, England, 1947 and Barclay Curle & Company Limited, Glasgow, Scotland, 1950 respectively. **Machinery** Doxford diesel, single screw. Speed 13½ knots. **Capacity** 13/26 first class, 41/60 second class, 1,050/500 deck class. Accommodation on the *Dwarka* revised as 62 saloon class and 1,020 deck in 1965. Continued in service until spring 1982, by then being final member of British India passenger fleet aside from the school-ship *Uganda* and also the last of their ships to be based abroad. Scrapped summer 1982 at Gadani Beach, Pakistan.

Daressa sold to the Chandris Group, Greek flag; delivered August 1964. Re-named *Favorita*. Intended conversion to Caribbean–Mediterranean cruise-ship with 600 berths never materialised; laid-up instead at Piraeus. Sold April 1968 to Guan Guan Shipping Company, Singapore; re-named *Kim Hwa*. Local Far Eastern service from Singapore. Engine breakdown at sea on July 2 1974; towed to Hong Kong. Uneconomic to repair; sold to local Hong Kong scrappers.

Sangola and *Sirdhana*

Service Calcutta to Rangoon, Penang, Singapore, Hong Kong, Yokohama and Kobe. **Particulars** 8,647/8,608 gross tons; 479 × 63 × 26 ft. **Builder** Barclay Curle & Company Limited, Glasgow, Scotland, 1947 and Swan, Hunter & Wigham Richardson Limited, Newcastle-upon-Tyne, England, 1947. **Machinery** Doxford diesels, twin screw. Speed 14½ knots. **Capacity** 21/21 first class, 34/32 second 'A' class, 30/30 second 'B' class, 335/333 bunked class, 995/987 deck class. **Notes** Both sister-ships to *Santhia*. *Sangola* sailed for British India until 1962. Sold to Japanese breakers in 1963. *Sirdhana* transferred to Persian Gulf service in 1963. Accommodation restyled as 92 saloon class, 729 bunked and 480 deck. Scrapped at Kaohsiung, Taiwan in late 1972.

Santhia

Service Bombay and Karachi to Persian Gulf ports (same as for *Dumra*). **Particulars** 8,908 gross tons; 479 ×63 × 26 ft. **Builder** Barclay Curle & Company Limited, Glasgow, Scotland, 1950. **Machinery** Doxford diesel, twin screw. Speed $14\frac{1}{2}$ knots. **Capacity** 25 first class, 70 second class, 68 intermediate class, 268 bunked class, 762 deck class. **Notes** Sister-ship to *Sangola* and *Sirdhana*. Sold in 1967 to Shipping Corporation of India, Indian flag, and re-named *State of Haryana* for passenger and pilgrim services. Major boiler problems at sea on June 5 1976; uneconomic to repair and laid-up. Fire damaged on January 3 1977 while anchored off Bombay awaiting demolition; later scrapped.

Mombasa

Service East African coastal run between Mombasa, Tanga, Zanzibar, Dar-es-Salaam, Lindi and Mtwara. **Particulars** 2,213 gross tons; 266 × 44 × 4 ft. **Builder** Henry Robb Limited, Leith, Scotland, 1950. **Machinery** British Polar diesels, twin screw. Speed $12\frac{1}{2}$ knots. **Capacity** 8 first class, 16 second class, 250 deck class. **Notes** Use of white hull discontinued soon after completion. Sailed for British India 1950–61. Sold in 1961 to Crescent Shipping Lines, Pakistani flag; re-named *Kareem*. Pilgrim and local services out of Karachi. No longer listed in 1973; disposition unknown.

Kampala

Service Bombay and Karachi to the Seychelles, Mombasa, Zanzibar, Dar-es-Salaam, Beira, Lourenco Marques and Durban. Periodic alterations in overall service and ports of call. **Particulars** 10,304 gross tons; 507 × 66 × 27 ft. **Builuer** Alexander Stephen & Sons Limited, Glasgow, Scotland, 1947. **Machinery:** Steam turbines, twin screw. Speed 16 knots. **Capacity** 60 first class, 180 second class, approximately 825 third class. **Notes** Sister-ship to *Karanja*. Maiden voyage to East Africa in August 1947. Sailed for British India until 1971, then scrapped in Taiwan.

Karanja

Service India–Pakistan–East Africa (same as for *Kampala*). **Particulars** 10,294 gross tons; 507 ×66 ×27 ft. **Builder** Alexander Stephen & Sons Limited, Glasgow, Scotland, 1948. **Machinery** Steam turbines, twin screw. Speed 16 knots. **Capacity** 60 first class, 180 second class, approximately 825 third class. **Notes** Sister-ship to *Kampala*. Maiden voyage October 1948. Major refit at Singapore in 1969. Laid-up at Bombay in June 1976; offered for sale. Later sold to Shipping Corporation of India, Indian flag, and re-named *Nancowry*. Indian local services and occasionally India to the Seychelles. Accommodation listed as 240 berthed and 800 deck passengers. Still in service.

Above left *Although briefly painted with a white hull the* Mombasa *reverted to the original black livery and retained this colouring to the very end of her British India days* (P&O Group).
Above *An aerial view showing the deck configuration of the* Karanja (P&O Group).
Below *P&O's* Chitral *and the* Karanja *together at Durban in 1969* (P&O Group).

Above *British India's flagship* Kenya *as seen in the English Channel* (P&O Group).

Kenya

Service London to Gibraltar and/or Malta, Port Said, Aden, Mombasa, Tanga, Zanzibar, Dar-es-Salaam and Beira. Homewards include Marseilles. **Particulars** 14,464 gross tones; 540 × 71 × 27 ft. **Builder** Barclay Curle & Company Limited, Glasgow, Scotland, 1951. **Machinery** Steam turbines, twin screw. Speed 16 knots. **Capacity** 194 first class, 103 tourist class. **Notes** *Kenya* and sister-ship *Uganda* were the largest British India passenger ships. *Kenya* left London on maiden voyage in August 1951. Hull colouring changed from black to white in 1955. Became one-class ship in 1965 with 297 berths. Thereafter all sailings terminated at Dar-es-Salaam. Arrived at London Docks on June 9 1969 and thereby terminated British India passenger service to Africa from British ports. Plan to convert *Kenya* to British industrial exhibition ship never materialised. Scrapped at La Spezia, Italy during summer 1969.

Uganda

Service London to East Africa (ports same as for *Kenya*). From 1968, educational cruising—both from British and Mediterranean ports (Piraeus, Naples, Malta, etc,). **Particulars** 14,430 gross tons; 540 × 71 × 27 ft. **Builder** Barclay Curle & Company Limited, Glasgow, Scotland, 1952. **Machinery** Steam turbines, twin screw. Speed 16 knots. **Capacity** 167 first class, 133 tourist class. **Notes** Maiden voyage August 1952. Given white hull in 1955. Withdrawn from East African run in December 1966. Sent to Hamburg and converted to educational cruise-ship. Accommodation restyled for 306 adults and 920 students. Tonnage re-listed as 16,907. Began educational cruises in February 1968. Highly successful and popular. Requisitioned by the British government on April 10 1982 for use as a hospital ship in the Falklands. Outfitted at Gibraltar. Released August 1982 and resumed educational cruises. Rechartered to the British government in January 1983 for use as relay and replenishment ship between Ascension and the Falklands. Charter extended into 1985. Now laid up awaiting disposal.

Nevasa

Service Government trooping until 1962—Medi-

Above *The* Uganda *as originally built with twin masts and smaller kingposts* (P&O Group).
Below Uganda *in more recent years as the vastly altered educational cruise-ship* (Michael Cassar).

Above *Triumph for the* Uganda*: Her official 'welcome home' from the Falklands in August 1982. Note the grey-hulled* Queen Elizabeth 2 *in the background, berthed at the Queen Elizabeth II Terminal at Southampton* (P&O Group).

Below *Following a full refit and restoration after her Falklands duty, the* Uganda *departs from Southampton on her first educational cruise, on September 28 1982. The* Sea Princess *of P&O is berthed in the background* (P&O Group).

Above *The* Nevasa *was British India's most popular educational cruise-ship* (Michael D. J. Lennon).
Below *A sad occasion:* Nevasa *outward bound from Malta for the breakers on Taiwan. She has been stripped of all but two of her lifeboats and she is flying her 'paying off' pennant* (Michael D. J. Lennon).

terranean, Middle and Far East, Africa, etc. 1965–75 used for educational cruising from British and Mediterranean ports. 1–3 week voyages. **Particulars** 20,527 gross tons; 609 × 78 × 26 ft. **Builder** Barclay Curle & Company Limited, Glasgow, Scotland, 1956. **Machinery** Steam turbines, twin screw. Speed 17½ knots. **Capacity** 220 first class, 100 second class, 180 third class, 1,000 troops. **Notes** Largest British India passenger-carrying vessel ever built. Began 15-year government trooping charter in July 1956. Charter cancelled in October 1962; ship laid-up in River Fal. Converted 1964–65 at Falmouth to educational cruise-ship. Accommodation restyled as 300 adult and 1,100 student passengers. Tonnage re-listed as 20,746. Resumed sailing in October 1965. Highly popular and successful. Became uneconomic during 1974 with increased fuel costs. Arrived at Kaohsiung, Taiwan on March 30 1975 for scrapping.

Canadian Pacific Steamships

Canadian Pacific Steamships inaugurated its trans-continental railway system across Canada in 1887. A transpacific passenger ship service, as an alternate route to Japan, Hong Kong and China, began two years later, and then was expanded to include a transatlantic service, between Liverpool and the St Lawrence River ports in 1903. For some years, in a giant consortium of interests, the company could advertise one of the largest transportation networks in the world, one which included not only ships, but trains, trucks, telegraph communications and later aircraft. The Pacific liner operation was not resumed after World War 2, while the Atlantic runs continued until 1971. The company's final passenger ship, the Canadian-flag *Princess Patricia*, which was used on the summer season Alaska cruise trade out of Vancouver, was retired in 1982.

Empress of France

Service Liverpool and Greenock to Quebec City and Montreal (to Saint John, New Brunswick in winter). **Particulars** 20,448 gross tons; 601 × 75 × 27 ft. **Builder** John Brown & Company Limited, Clydebank, Scotland, 1928. **Machinery** Steam turbines, twin screw. Speed 18 knots. **Capacity** 218 first class, 482 tourist class. **Notes** Maiden voyage June 1928 as *Duchess of Bedford* for Canadian Pacific. Chartered to Furness–Bermuda Lines during 1933 for New York–Bermuda

Canadian Pacific's last trio of great Atlantic liners: the Empress of Britain *of 1956* **below left,** *her twin sister-ship, the* Empress of England *of 1957* **above,** *and finally, the modified and larger* Empress of Canada *of 1961* **below** (Roger Sherlock; Alex Duncan; Richard K. Morse collection).

Canadian Pacific's regal Empress of France *as seen in her final days in 1959—60 with her modernised funnels* (Roger Sherlock).

cruises. Requisitioned for trooping in August 1939. Decommissioned from war duties in 1947. Major refit 1947–48. Resumed Canadian Pacific sailings as *Empress of France* (original intention was to re-name her as *Empress of India*) in September 1948. Carried Princess Elizabeth and the Duke of Edinburgh to Canada in autumn 1951. Major refit in 1959; given new streamlined funnels. Retired at Liverpool in December 1960. Soon afterward, scrapped at Newport, Monmouthshire.

Empress of Britain

Service Summer season service between Liverpool, Greenock, Quebec City and Montreal. Winter sailings to Saint John, New Brunswick or cruising from New York. **Particulars** 25,516 gross tons; 640 × 85 × 29 ft. **Builder** Fairfield Shipbuilding & Engineering Company, Glasgow, Scotland, 1956. **Machinery** Steam turbines, twin screw. Speed 20 knots. **Capacity** 160 first class, 894 tourist class; 650 one-class for cruises. **Notes** First British liner to be completely air-conditioned. Launched by Her Majesty Queen Elizabeth II on June 22 1955. Maiden voyage April 1956. Offered for sale February 1964. Sold to Goulandris Group, Greek flag and delivered in January 1965. Rebuilt at Genoa as *Queen Anna Maria* for Greek Line transatlantic service to New York. Capacity increased to 1,254 berths and tonnage re-listed as 21,716. Grounded off Kingston, Jamaica on February 19 1967; later refloated. Terminated Greek Line passenger operations in January 1975. Laid-up at Perama, Greece. Sold to Carnival Cruise Lines, Panama flag, in December 1975. Re-named *Carnivale* for Miami–Caribbean cruising. Still in service.

Empress of England

Service North Atlantic to Canada (same as for *Empress of Britain*). **Particulars** 25,585 gross tons; 640 × 85 × 29 ft. **Builder** Vickers-Armstrong Shipbuilders Limited, Newcastle-upon-Tyne, England, 1957. **Machinery** Steam turbines, twin screw. Speed 20 knots. **Capacity** 160 first class, 898 tourist class; 650 one-class when cruising. **Notes** Sister-ship to *Empress of Britain*. Maiden voyage April 1957. Collision off Quebec City in November 1965 with Norwegian tanker. Sold in April 1970 to Shaw Savill Line; re-named *Ocean Monarch (qv)*.

Empress of Canada

Service North Atlantic to Canada and cruising (same as for *Empress of Britain*). **Particulars** 27,284 gross tons; 650 × 87 × 29 ft. **Builder** Vickers-Armstrong

Shipbuilders Limited, Newcastle-upon-Tyne, England, 1961. **Machinery** Steam turbines, twin screw. Speed 20 knots. **Capacity** 200 first class, 856 tourist class; 650 one-class for cruises. **Notes** Last Canadian Pacific passenger liner. Maiden voyage April 1961. Rumoured to become *Dominion Monarch* for Shaw Savill in December 1970; never materialised. Withdrawn November 1971, closing-out Canadian Pacific North Atlantic service. Sold in January 1972 to Carnival Cruise Lines, Panama flag, and re-named *Mardi Gras* for Miami-Caribbean cruising. Still in service.

Cunard Line

The Cunard Line has probably been the best known name in passenger shipping. Its interests, however, have been largely restricted to the North Atlantic, particularly to New York. First organised in 1838, the first regular sailings, to Halifax and Boston, began two years later. Steady growth and prosperity followed, resulting in some of the most notable liners of all time. The likes of the four-funnel *Mauretania, Lusitania* and *Aquitania* led eventually to the illustrious *Queen Mary* and *Queen Elizabeth*, the best known and most successful pair of superliners ever built. In fact, the *Elizabeth* still ranks as the largest liner ever built.

Hard hit by the intrusion of aircraft that began in the late '50s and then the gradual transition to specialised cruise-ships, the company's position has declined in recent years and is now comparable to many other leisure sailing firms. A division of the Trafalgar House Group, the *Queen Elizabeth 2*, the last of the superliners and the last on the traditional Atlantic run to New York, heads a fleet of cruise-ships that includes the *Cunard Countess* and the Bahamas-registered *Cunard Princess*. In 1983, Cunard acquired Norwegian America Cruises and their two liners, the *Sagafjord* and *Vistafjord*, but both ships were placed under Bahamian colours.

A most unusual aerial view, just above New York's 'Luxury Liner Row.' Dated April 7 1959, it includes (from left to right) a US Navy cruiser, the Giulio Cesare, United States, Liberte, Ivernia, Queen Mary, Mauretania *(just sailing) and the* Media (Richard K. Morse collection).

Above *The last of the White Star liners, the* Britannic, *wore her original funnel colours throughout her Cunard career until 1960* (Alex Duncan).
Above right *The* Queen Mary *painted in wartime grey serving as a heroic trooper. Here at anchor off Gourock* (Imperial War Museum).
Below right *The last of the North Atlantic's three-stackers, the* Queen Mary *gracefully enters New York's Hudson River* (Cunard).

Britannic

Service Liverpool and Cobh to New York. Annual winter cruise from New York to the Mediterranean and Black Seas. **Particulars** 27,666 gross tons; 712 × 82 × 35 ft. **Builder** Harland & Wolff Limited, Belfast, Northern Ireland, 1930. **Machinery** Burmeister & Wain diesels, twin screw. Speed 18 knots. **Capacity** 429 first class and 564 tourist class. **Notes** Last ship to wear original White Star Line colours. Maiden voyage for White Star in June 1930. Acquired as part of Cunard-White Star merger in 1934. 1939–47 wartime trooping. Resumed commercial service May 1948. Collided with American freighter *Pioneer Land* in New York Harbour on June 1 1950; repaired. Broken crankshaft with forced lay-up at New York in summer 1960. Sold for scrapping at Inverkeithing, Scotland in December 1960.

Queen Mary

Service Weekly express run with *Queen Elizabeth* between Southampton, Cherbourg and New York. **Particulars** 81,237 gross tons; 1,019 × 119 × 39 ft. **Builder** John Brown & Company Limited, Clydebank, Scotland, 1930–36. **Machinery** Steam turbines, quadruple screw. Speed 28½ knots. **Capacity** 711 first class, 707 cabin class and 577 tourist class. **Notes** World's fastest liner 1938–52. First major Cunarder to dispense with 'ia' name ending; last three-funnel liner. Keel laid December 27 1930 but construction halted December 1931 until April 1934. Launched by Her Majesty Queen Mary on September 26 1934. Maiden voyage May 1936. Firmly took Atlantic Blue Riband from French *Normandie* in August 1938 with record speed of 31.6 knots. 1939–46 used as a wartime troop-ship. Rammed and sank British cruiser HMS *Curacoa* off Northern Ireland on October 2 1942; 338 casualties. Sailed with 16,683 troops and crew aboard in July 1943, the greatest number ever for any ship. Refitted 1946–47. Resumed Atlantic sailings July 1947. First cruise in December 1963; Southampton to Las Palmas. Rumoured in 1967 to become Australian immigrant ship and later New York City school-ship. Made final sailing from New York on September 22 1967. Sold to City of Long Beach, California for over $3 million. Extensively rebuilt for use as a hotel and museum-ship. Renovations cost over $70 million. Opened to the public on May 8 1971. Given improvements in 1980. Still in use.

Left *A poetic photograph of the* Queen Mary, *heading for the open Atlantic on a winter's afternoon in the late 1950s* (The Port Authority of New York & New Jersey).
Above *The* Queen Mary*'s three distinctive funnels were a well known sight to both Southampton and New York. In this especially evocative view, taken at New York on February 7 1953, a low-hanging fog obscured all but the upper portions of the ship* (Frank O. Braynard collection).
Below *Hail and farewell: the* Queen Mary *leaving Southampton for the last time, in October 1967* (Victor Scrivens collection).

Above *The* Queen Mary *in retirement in southern California, as a hotel-ship, museum and array of shops and restaurants* (Hotel Queen Mary).
Above right *A modified, smaller version of the giant* Queen Elizabeth, *the* Mauretania *of 1939 was a particularly beloved Cunarder. She is seen here in-bound at New York steaming up the Hudson River with the Anchor Line freighter* Sidonia *in the foreground. The view dates from 1960* (Richard K. Morse collection).
Below right *One of the grandest and greatest Cunarders: the second* Mauretania *about to be docked at her New York pier* (Everett E. Viez collection).

Mauretania

Service Southampton, Le Havre, and Cobh to New York. Winter cruising from New York to the Caribbean. **Particulars** 35,655 gross tons; 772 × 89 × 30 ft. **Builder** Cammell Laird & Company Limited, Birkenhead, England, 1939. **Machinery** Steam turbines, twin screw. Speed 23 knots. **Capacity** 470 first class, 370 cabin class and 300 tourist class. **Notes** Maiden voyage June 1939. 1939–46 used for wartime trooping. Refitted 1946–47. Resumed Atlantic sailings in June 1947. Repainted in green in December 1962 and used mostly for cruising. Used during 1963 for experimental service between Mediterranean and New York; unsuccessful. Retired in November 1965. Scrapped at Inverkeithing, Scotland.

Queen Elizabeth

Service Express run with *Queen Mary* between Southampton, Cherbourg and New York. **Particulars** 83,673 gross tons; 1,031 × 119 × 39 ft. **Builder** John Brown & Company Limited, Clydebank, Scotland, 1936–40. **Machinery** Steam turbines, quadruple screw. Speed 28½ knots. **Capacity** 823 first class, 662 cabin class and 798 tourist class. **Notes** The largest liner ever built. Laid down December 1936. Launched by Her Majesty Queen Elizabeth (later the Queen Mother) on September 27 1938. Darted for safety of New York in winter 1940. 1940–46 used as a wartime trooper; with totals of 800,000 passengers and 500,000 miles steamed. 1946—refitted for commercial service. Maiden voyage October 1946. Aground at Bramble Bank for 24 hours in 1947. Collided with tug at New York in December 1952; minor damages. Carried Her Majesty Queen Elizabeth the Queen Mother as a passenger in autumn 1954. Collision outside New York Harbour with American freighter *American Hunter* in August 1959. Refit in late 1960. Extensive three-month refit in 1965–66. Tonnage relisted as 82,998. Final Cunard sailing in November 1968. Record of 907 Atlantic crossings, 3.4 million miles and 2.3 million

Left *The world's largest liner, the 83,673-ton* Queen Elizabeth, *resting in the King George V Graving Dock at Southampton during her annual winter overhaul* (Cunard).
Above *The great Cunarders were almost always included in the spectacular gatherings of transatlantic liners at the New York City docks. The* Queen Elizabeth *is just arriving, with the* United States *and* Constitution *in the background* (Cunard).
Below *Five liners berthed together on an otherwise hazy summer's day. The* Queen Elizabeth *is in the nearest berth, prominently featured, with (left to right) the* America, United States, Ile de France *and* Georgic *at other slips* (The Port Authority of New York & New Jersey).

Left *A flotilla of tugs manoeuvre the giant* Queen Elizabeth *at Southampton at the time of her post-war refit in the late summer of 1946* (Captain Eric Ashton-Irvine collection).
Above *Floodlit and majestic the* Queen Elizabeth *at the Southampton Ocean Terminal with the bow of P&O's* Iberia *to the right* (J. K. Byass).
Below *The original Cunard black hull is changed gradually to white as the world's largest passenger ship is converted to the* Seawise University, *a cruise-ship floating university, at Hong Kong during the autumn of 1971* (James L. Shaw collection).

Above *Scorched and capsized, the remains of the former* Queen Elizabeth *at Hong Kong in the spring of 1972* (J. T. Gibbons, from the collection of Everett E. Viez).
Above right *The* Media *and her twin sister-ship, the* Parthia, *were Cunard's only post-war combination passenger-cargo liners on the North Atlantic* (Richard K. Morse collection).
Below right *Hardly recognisable following her 1961—62 refit, the former* Media *as the Italian immigrant ship* Flavia (Roger Sherlock).

passengers. Sent to Port Everglades, Florida to become museum and hotel-ship. Never materialised; later bankrupt. Auctioned off in September 1970 to C. Y. Tung Group. Re-named *Seawise University* for conversion to university and cruise-ship. Refitted at Hong Kong. Just prior to completion, caught fire and capsized in Hong Kong harbour on January 8th–9th 1972. Later scrapped on the spot.

Media and *Parthia*

Service Liverpool direct to New York. Occasionally via Norfolk, Bermuda or Greenock. **Particulars** 13,345/13,362 gross tons respectively; 531 × 70 × 30 ft. **Builder** John Brown & Company Limited, Clydebank, Scotland, 1947 and Harland & Wolff Limited, Belfast, Northern Ireland, 1948 respectively. **Machinery** Steam turbines, twin screw. Speed 18 knots. **Capacity** 250 first class. **Notes** *Media* was the first brand-new post-war Atlantic liner and later the first Atlantic ship to be fitted with stabilizers. Both intended to be Brocklebank Line freighters, but redesigned for Cunard in early construction phases. *Media* maiden voyage in August 1947. Fitted with stabilisers in January 1953. Sold in 1961 to Cogedar Line, Italian flag and re-named *Flavia.* Rebuilt for Australian immigrant trade with 1,320 berths. Lengthened to 557 ft. Began sailing in December 1962. Transferred to the Costa Line in 1968 for Miami–Bahamas crusing. Engine breakdown in the Caribbean in October 1974; later repaired. Sold in February 1982 to Chinese interests; laid-up at Hong Kong. Still afloat. *Parthia* sailed for Cunard until 1961, then sold to New Zealand Shipping Company and re-named *Remuera (qv).*

MEDIA

FLAVIA

Being painted in several shades of very distinctive green, Cunard's Caronia *was known affectionately as 'the Green Goddess'* (Roger Sherlock).

Caronia

Service Near-continuous cruising from New York: Around-the-world, Pacific or around Africa in January; Mediterranean in spring; North Cape–Scandinavia in June; Mediterranean in fall. Occasional sailings between Southampton, Le Havre and New York. **Particulars** 34,172 gross tons; 715 × 91 × 31 ft. **Builder** John Brown & Company Limited, Clydebank, Scotland, 1948. **Machinery** Steam turbines, twin screw. Speed 22 knots. **Capacity** 581 first class and 351 cabin class; 600 one-class for cruises. **Notes** In 1949, largest liner yet built purposely for cruising; also, largest single-funnel liner yet built. Launched by Princess Elizabeth on October 30 1947. Maiden voyage January 1949. Rammed lighthouse at Yokohama on April 14 1958. Major refit late 1965. Laid-up November 1967. Intended to become Yugoslavian hotel-ship in 1968; never materialised. Sold to Universal Line, Panamanian flag, in May 1968 and refitted as cruise-ship *Caribia.* Cruising from New York. Engine room explosion in Caribbean on March 5 1969. Towed back to New York; laid-up until 1974. Rumoured to be sold to C. Y. Tung Group, then Lauro Line; never materialised. Left New York on April 27 1974 under tow for Taiwan scrapyards. Wrecked at Guam on August 12; later dismantled on the spot.

Saxonia/Carmania and *Ivernia/Franconia*

Service Southampton and Le Havre to Quebec City and Montreal; occasionally included Rotterdam and Cobh. Winter sailings to Halifax and New York. Later full-time cruising for both ships. **Particulars** 21,637/21,717 gross tons respectively; 608 × 80 × 28 ft. **Builder** John

In the last years of their Cunard service the Carmania *and her sister-ship* Franconia *were painted all-white* (Michael Cassar).

Brown & Company Limited, Clydebank, Scotland, 1954 and 1955 respectively. **Machinery** Steam turbines, twin screw. Speed 19½ knots. **Capacity** 125 first class and 800 tourist class. **Notes** Two of four identical sister-ships—*Saxonia, Ivernia, Carinthia* and *Sylvania. Saxonia* launched by Lady Churchill on February 17 1954. Maiden voyage September 1954. Major refit 1962–63 for increased cruise service; re-named *Carmania.* Accommodation restyled as 117 first class and 764 tourist class. Repainted in green colouring. Repainted in white in 1967. Aground in the Bahamas on January 12–13 1969; later repaired. Collision with Soviet tanker off Gibraltar on May 14 1969. Hull damaged in the Caribbean in March 1970. Laid-up December 1971; rumoured to be sold to Greek Chandris Group, then Japanese interests. Sold August 1973 to Black Sea Steamship Company, Soviet flag, becoming the *Leonid Sobinov.* Cruising and Southampton–Australia sailings. Being used in 1980 by Cuban government for troop service. Resumed cruise sailings late 1981.

Ivernia maiden voyage July 1955. Major refit 1962–63 for increased cruise service. Re-named *Franconia.* Repainted in green, accommodation re-styled as 119 first class and 728 tourist class and tonnage relisted as 22,637. Repainted in white in 1967 and transferred to New York–Bermuda service. Laid-up December 1971. Rumoured to be sold to Chandris Lines, then Japanese interests. Sold August 1973 to Black Sea Steamship Company, Soviet flag, and re-named *Feodor Shalyapin.* Cruising and Southampton–Australia sailings. Being used during 1980 for troop service between Havana and the Middle East and East Africa. Resumed cruise sailings in late 1981.

FRANCONIA

Carinthia and *Sylvania*

Service Liverpool and Greenock to Quebec City and Montreal during ice-free season; Liverpool and Cobh to Halifax and New York during winter months. **Particulars** 21,947 gross tons; 608 × 80 × 28 ft. **Builder** John Brown & Company Limited, Clydebank, Scotland, 1956 and 1957 respectively. **Machinery** Steam turbines, twin screw. Speed $19\frac{1}{2}$ knots. **Capacity** 154 first class and 714 tourist class. **Notes** Original sister-ships to *Saxonia* and *Ivernia*. *Carinthia* launched by Princess Margaret on December 14 1955. Maiden voyage June 1956. Hull repainted in white in 1967. Made final Cunard passenger sailing to Canada in October 1967; then laid-up at Southampton. Sold May 1968 to Sitmar Line, Liberian flag, and re-named *Fairland*, then *Fairsea*. 1968–70 idle at Southampton. 1970–71 rebuilt at Trieste for North American cruising. Accommodation restyled as 910 first class and tonnage re-listed as 21,916. Entered Sitmar cruise service December 1971. Damaged while in dry-dock at Alameda, California in September 1976; repaired. Still in service.

Sylvania entered service June 1957. Transferred to year-round Liverpool–Cobh–New York run in April 1961. Made first Cunard cruise from Liverpool since 1939 in October 1964. Terminated Cunard's Liverpool–New York service in November 1966. Repainted in white in December 1966. Laid-up May 1968. Sold to Sitmar Line, Liberian flag, and re-named *Fairwind*. 1968–70 remained idle at Southampton. 1970–71 rebuilt at Trieste as a cruise-ship: accommodation restyled as 910 first class and tonnage re-listed as 21,985. Entered North American cruise service July 1972. Fire and engine room damaged while in the Caribbean in November 1975; repaired. Still in service.

Left *Between 1967-71 Cunard ran a special seasonal cruise service between New York and Hamilton, Bermuda using the* Franconia (Cunard).
Below *The* Carinthia *and her other twin sister-ships were the last Cunarders built for the Canadian trade* (Roger Sherlock).

Top *For about two years, the* Fairwind, *the former* Sylvania *(left), and the* Fairland, *ex*-Carinthia, *were laid-up abreast of one another at the Southampton Docks. In the far distance are the* S. A. Vaal *and* Canberra (World Ship Society Photo Library).
Above *Almost unrecognisable, the former* Carinthia *seen as the rebuilt* Fairsea (Roger Sherlock).

Queen Elizabeth 2

Service Southampton and Cherbourg to New York with considerable cruising, 2–90 days. **Particulars** 65,863 gross tons; 963 × 105 × 32 ft. **Builder** John Brown & Company Limited, Clydebank, Scotland, 1965–69. **Machinery** Steam turbines, twin screw. Speed 28½ knots. **Capacity** 564 first class and 1,441 tourist class; 1,400 one-class for cruises. **Notes** Last great Atlantic superliner. Laid down June 1965 and launched by Her Majesty Queen Elizabeth II on September 20 1967. Trials late 1968; defects and Cunard refused delivery until spring 1969. Averaged 32.66 knots. Maiden voyage to New York in May 1969. Rescued survivors from burning French liner *Antilles* in the Caribbean on January 9 1971. Capacity restyled as

Top *The last of the transatlantic superliners, the* Queen Elizabeth 2 (Roger Sherlock).
Above *The* QE2*'s return from duty in the South Atlantic, during the Falklands crisis, in June 1983* (Southern Newspapers Limited).

604 first class and 1,223 tourist class in 1972. 1,740 one-class for cruising.

Immobilised by boiler troubles off Bermuda on April 1 1974. 1,630 passengers transferred to nearby *Sea Venture* on April 3. Boiler trouble during Mediterranean cruise in September 1974. Blown against pier at Cherbourg on October 28 1974. Damaged hull at Nassau in December 1975. Engine room fire at sea on July 23 1976. Capacity restyled as 1,820 for all sailings. New suites added late 1977 and tonnage relisted as 67,107 tons. Damaged in North Atlantic storm in September 1978. Extensive refit at New York in late 1979. Requisitioned by British government for service in the Falklands on May 3 1982. Resumed regular service August 1982. Major refit in summer 1983. Conversion to diesel-electric planned for 1986–87.

The enormous bow of the QE2 *while undergoing a major refit at the Hapag-Lloyd Shipyards at Bremerhaven in December 1983* (Hapag-Lloyd Shipyards).

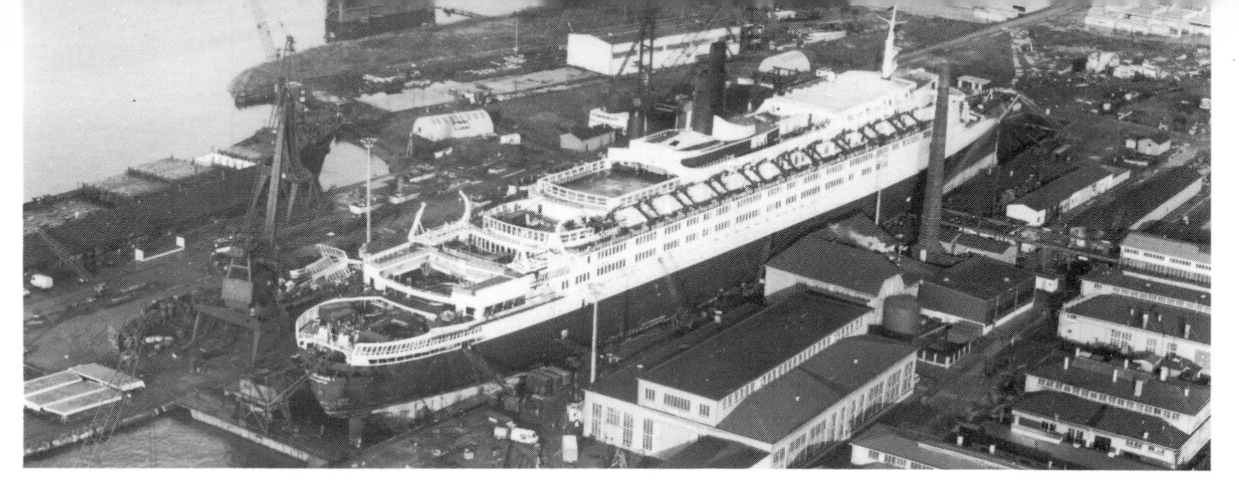

Cunard Adventurer* and *Cunard Ambassador
Service Mostly seven-day Caribbean cruises from San Juan, Puerto Rico. Also sailings from Port Everglades, Norfolk and from New York to Bermuda. **Particulars** 14,155 gross tons; 484 × 71 × 19 ft. **Builder** Rotterdam Drydock Company, Rotterdam, Holland, 1971 and 1972 respectively. **Machinery** Stork-Werkspor diesels, twin screw. Speed 20½ knots. **Capacity** 806 first class. **Notes** Both ordered originally by Overseas National Airways, then Cunard had 50 per cent interest and finally full ownership. *Adventurer* maiden voyage December 1971. Engine room fire in the Caribbean on July 3 1974; later repaired. Mechanical problems during 1975. Collision at San Juan with Costa liner *Carla C.* on February 14 1976. Late 1976 rumoured to become Hawaiian cruise-ship; never materialised. Sold in November 1976 to Norwegian Caribbean Lines, Norwegian flag, and re-named *Sunward II* for Miami–Bahamas crusing. Major refit 1976–77. Entered service May 1977.

Cunard Ambassador maiden voyage October 1972. Engine breakdown off Venezuela in June 1974. Heavily damaged by fire off Florida on September 15 1974. Beyond economic repair and sold to C. Clausen A/S, Danish flag. Rebuilt 1975–76 as sheep carrier *Linda Clausen*. Capacity for 30,000 sheep on Australia–Middle East service. Sold in 1980 to Qatar Transport and Marine Services Co, Qatar flag, and re-named *Procyon* and then *Raslan*. Engine room fire on July 3 1984 while sailing from Jeddah to Singapore. Uneconomic to repair; scrapped at Kaohsiung during autumn 1984.

Above *Undergoing a large refit, especially to her aft pool deck area, the* QE2 *is seen in dry-dock at Bremerhaven in December 1983* (Hapag-Lloyd Shipyards).
Below *Following a fire off the Florida coast the* Cunard Ambassador *was sold off to the Danish Clausen interests and rebuilt as an Australian sheep carrier* (Cunard).

Above *The* Cunard Countess *at her year round base, San Juan in Puerto Rico* (Cunard).

Above right *Curnow's little* St Helena *restored South African passenger service following the withdrawl of Union-Castle* (Roger Sherlock).

Right *Donaldson's* Lismoria *in her final year berthed at Boston while making some cargo voyages under charter to Cunard* (Michael Cassar).

Cunard Countess and *Cunard Princess*

Service Cruising—Caribbean from San Juan, Alaska from Vancouver and Mexico from Los Angeles. **Particulars** 17,495 gross tons; 536 × 74 × 18 ft. **Builder** Burmeister & Wain Shipyards, Copenhagen, Denmark and then outfitted by Industrie Navali Merchaniche Affine Shipyard, La Spezia, Italy, 1976 and 1977 respectively. **Machinery** Burmeister & Wain diesels, twin screw. Speed $20\frac{1}{2}$ knots. **Capacity** 750 first class. **Notes** *Cunard Countess* maiden voyage August 1976. Used by British government in spring 1983 for South Atlantic service to the Falklands; followed by major refit in Malta. *Cunard Princess* was launched as *Cunard Conquest*, but re-named prior to completion. Shipyard fire on April 14 1976. Named at New York in March 1977 by Princess Grace of Monaco. Chartered to Lauro Lines for Mediterranean cruising June–November 1979. Resumed Cunard service in December 1979. Transferred to Bahamas flag in October 1980.

Curnow Shipping Limited

Curnow Shipping Limited was formed in 1977 and, acquiring a small former Alaskan coastal passenger ship, had her refitted for South Atlantic service. Primarily providing a vital link to the island of St Helena, voyages continue to Cape Town before turning around and have therefore filled somewhat the void left when Union Castle abandoned passenger liner service.

St Helena

Service Avonmouth to Cape Town via Las Palmas, Ascension and Jamestown. **Particulars** 3,150 gross tons; 321 × 46 × 16 ft. **Builder** Burrard Drydock Company, Vancouver, British Columbia, 1963. **Machinery** Diesel, single screw. Speed $16\frac{1}{2}$ knots. **Capacity** 88 one-class. **Notes** Built as *Northland Prince* for Northland Navigation Company, Canadian flag, for Alaska coastal service from Vancouver. Sold to Curnow Shipping in 1977 and changed to British flag. Given refit. Maiden voyage to South Atlantic in September 1978. Chartered to British government in May 1982 for Falklands service; released in summer 1983. Resumed commercial sailings autumn 1983.

Donaldson Line

The Donaldson Line was first organised in 1855, but did not begin Atlantic crossings to eastern Canada until 1876. The company's last combination passenger-cargo ships were retired in 1966, and shortly thereafter the entire firm was disbanded.

Laurentia and *Lismoria*

Service Glasgow direct to Montreal (to Saint John, New Brunswick and Halifax in winter). **Particulars** 8,323/8,349 gross tons respectively; 455 × 62 × 28 ft. **Builder** California Shipbuilding Corporation, Los Angeles, California, 1945 and Permanente Shipyard No 1, Richmond, California, 1945 respectively. **Machinery** Steam turbines, single screw. Speed 15 knots. **Capacity** 55 first class. **Notes** Former Victory Class freighters *Taos Victory* and *Medina Victory* respectively. Given to Britain in 1946 and rebuilt for Donaldson in 1948–49. Used as freighters during winter sailings beginning in 1961. Both withdrawn from Donaldson service in late 1966, then used briefly as freighters. *Laurentia* scrapped in Taiwan in summer 1967 and *Lismoria* broken-up in Spain in winter 1967.

Elder Dempster Lines

Elder Dempster Lines is assuredly the best known British shipping company trading to West Africa. 'ED'—as it was often called—began by taking over the very early African Steam Navigation Company, in 1881, and then the British & African Steam Navigation Company. Passenger sailings were begun at about the same time, in the 1880s. The Elder Dempster name was adopted formally in 1932, and for a time thereafter came under Blue Funnel management. While the final passenger sailing took place in 1974, the firm remains involved heavily in freight shipping.

Calabar and *Winneba*

Service London to Madeira, Freetown, Takoradi, Lagos and Apapa. **Particulars** 8,305/8,355 gross tons respectively; 468 × 61 × 25 ft. **Builder** Swan, Hunter & Wigham Richardson Limited, Newcastle, England, 1936 and 1938 respectively. **Machinery** Steam triple expansion engines, twin screw. Speed 13½ knots. **Capacity** 105 first class passengers. **Notes** Both built originally for Natal Line service to South & East Africa; known as *Umtali* and *Umtata* respectively. 1939–46 war service. *Umtata* heavily damaged in London Blitz in September 1940; later repaired. Resumed sailings for Natal Line until 1957, then sold to Elder Dempster and re-named for West African service. Both withdrawn December 1962. *Calabar* scrapped in Inverkeithing, Scotland in early 1963. *Winneba* made final Elder Dempster passenger sailing from London and then scrapped at Antwerp in winter 1963.

Tarkwa and *Tamele*

Service Liverpool to various West African ports, determined by cargo requirements. **Particulars** 7,414/7,173 gross tons; 460/451 × 59 × 26 ft respectively. **Builders** Caledon Shipbuilding & Engineering Company, Dundee, Scotland, 1944 and Cammell Laird & Company Limited, Birkenhead, England, 1945 respectively. **Machinery** Diesel, single/twin screw. Speed 13¼ knots. **Capacity** 40 first class, 32 third class and just 36 first class respectively. **Notes** Built as wartime freighter-transports. Sailed for Elder Dempster until late 1966. Both sold to Guan Guan

Below *The* Winneba *and her sister-ship* Calabar *were the last Elder Dempster passenger ships to sail from the Port of London* (Alex Duncan).

Above right *The* Tarkwa *and her near sister-ship, the* Tamele, *were actually wartime transports that were modified for post-war commercial service by Elder Dempster* (World Ship Society Photo Library).

Below right *The* Apapa *continued in service after her sale by Elder Dempster as the Far Eastern based* Taiphooshan *for Hong Kong owners* (J. K. Byass).

Shipping Company, Singapore, for Far Eastern service. *Tarkwa* re-named as *Golden Lion*, *Tamele* as *Golden City*. *Golden Lion* scrapped at Shanghai in 1971 and *Golden City* at Hong Kong in 1973.

Accra and *Apapa*

Service Liverpool to Las Palmas, Freetown, Takoradi, Lagos and Apapa. **Particulars** 11,644/11,651 gross tons respectively; 471 × 66 × 25 ft. **Builder** Vickers Armstrong Shipbuilders Limited, Barrow-in-Furness, England, 1947 and 1948 respectively. **Machinery** Doxford diesels, twin screw. Speed 15½ knots. **Capacity** 259 first class and 24 third class. **Notes** *Accra* had maiden voyage in September 1947, *Apapa* in March 1948. *Accra* retired in October 1967 and sold to Spanish breakers at Cartagena. *Apapa* withdrawn in September 1968 and sold to Chun Sheong Steam Navigation Company, Hong Kong; re-named *Taiphooshan*. Local services from Hong Kong. Scrapped on Taiwan in winter 1975.

Aureol
Service Liverpool to Las Palmas, Freetown, Takoradi, Lagos and Apapa. **Particulars** 14,083 gross tons; 537 × 70 × 25 ft. **Builder** Alexander Stephen & Sons Limited, Glasgow, Scotland, 1951. **Machinery** Doxford diesels, twin screw. Speed 16 knots. **Capacity** 253 first class, 76 cabin class and 24 interchangeable. **Notes** Elder Dempster flagship and final passenger ship. Maiden voyage November 1951. Made first Elder Dempster cruise in December 1967. Began sailing from Southampton in April 1972, thereby ending company's Liverpool passenger operations. Withdrawn October 1974. Rumoured to be sold to Pakistani buyers; never materialised. Sold instead to John S. Latsis Line, Greek flag. Re-named *Marianna VI*. Laid-up Piraeus. Used at Jeddah as hotel-ship March 1976 until February 1979. Then laid-up in Perama Bay, Greece. Returned to Saudi Arabia for further use as a hotel-ship in February 1980. Still in use.

Elders & Fyffes Ltd

Elders & Fyffes Limited has long been established as one of the world's foremost banana and tropical fruit shippers. Initially formed with both British and American capital in 1901, it became a wholly-owned subsidiary of the US-based United Fruit Company in 1910. The Fyffes ships did retain their British registry, however. Passenger service ended completely by the '70s and the remaining fleet was sold off.

Golfito
Service Southampton or Avonmouth to Barbados, Trinidad, Kingston and occasionally Bermuda. **Particulars** 8,740 gross tons; 447 × 62 × 26 ft. **Builder** Alexander Stephen & Sons Limited, Glasgow, Scotland, 1949. **Machinery** Steam turbines, twin screw. Speed 17½ knots. **Capacity** 111 first class passengers. **Notes** Passenger-carrying 'banana boat' and near-sister to later *Camito*. Scrapped 1971 at Faslane, Scotland.

Camito
Service Same West Indies service as for *Golfito*. **Particulars** 8,687 gross tons; 448 × 62 × 26 ft. **Builder** Alexander Stephen & Sons Limited, Glasgow, Scotland, 1956. **Machinery** Steam turbines, twin screw. Speed 17½ knots. **Capacity** 113 first class. **Notes** Near-sister to earlier *Golfito*. Laid-up at Southampton in June 1972. Scrapped on Taiwan in spring 1973.

Above left *The* Aureol *closed out Elder Dempster's passenger services to West Africa in the autumn of 1974* (Roger Sherlock). *The last of the Elders & Fyffes 'banana boats' that carried more than a dozen passengers: the* Golfito **below** *and* Camito **above** (Both, Roger Sherlock).

Above *One fourth of a handsome quartet, the* City of Exeter *and her sister-ships of the Ellerman & Bucknall Lines each had five cargo holds* (Alex Duncan).
Top right *Although the* City of Durban *was never converted for Greek ferry-cruise service, her basic design can be compared to the* Mediterranean Sea *and therein reaffirm the changes that can take place at the hands of shipyard crews* (Roger Sherlock).
Right *The former* City of Exeter *as the totally rebuilt* Mediterranean Sea—*a futuristic looking Greek-registered liner* (Karageorgis Lines).

Ellerman & Bucknall Lines

Ellerman & Bucknall Lines was first created in 1914, through the acquisition of the Bucknall Steamship Lines by the important, ever-growing Ellerman Group. Created late last century by Sir John Ellerman, the Ellerman Company has extended rapidly into one of the world's largest shipping organisations. The additional acquisition soon thereafter of the City Line prompted the subsequent Ellerman naming theme, which has continued to the present day. The final passenger ships, the *City of Port Elizabeth* and her three sisters, were retired in 1971, and the company's trading thereafter limited to cargo ships.

City of Port Elizabeth, City of Exeter, City of York and *City of Durban*

Service London (and other North European ports such as Hamburg, Rotterdam, Antwerp, etc) to Las Palmas, Cape Town, Port Elizabeth, East London, Durban, Lourenco Marques and Beira. **Particulars** 13,363/ 13,345/13,345/13,345 gross tons respectively; 541 × 71 × 28 ft. **Builder** Vickers Armstrong Shipbuilders Limited, Newcastle, England, 1952/1953/1953/1954 respectively. **Machinery** Doxford diesels, twin screw. Speed 16½ knots. **Capacity** 107 first class. **Notes** Four identical sister-ships. *City of Port Elizabeth* was first of the group and entered service January 1953. *City of York* closed out Ellerman passenger service in June 1971. Four ships laid-up and then sold.

All sold to Karageorgis Group, Greek flag. *City of Port Elizabeth* re-named *Mediterranean Island* and then laid-up at Kalamata, Greece pending decision on future use. Re-named *Mediterranean Sun* in 1976, but still unused. Rumoured to be rebuilt in 1977 as cruise-ship-ferry. Left Piraeus under tow of tug *Amsterdam* on March 12 1980, bound for Kaohsiung, Taiwan scrapyards.

City of Exeter rebuilt 1971–72 as ferry *Mediterranean Sea.* Entered Adriatic service in December 1972. Accommodation restyled for 830 passengers and 300 vehicles. Tonnage re-listed as 15,212 tons. Transferred from Greek to Cypriot registry in 1974 and tonnage re-listed as 16,384. Temporarily used as a trade-fair ship in the Middle East in fall 1978, then resumed Mediterranean service. Still in operation.

City of York eventually rebuilt as ferry-cruise-ship *Mediterranean Sky.* Accommodation for 850 passengers and 340 vehicles. Tonnage re-listed as 14,941. Began Aegean service in June 1974.

City of Durban re-named as *Mediterranean Dolphin*, but never used. Scrapped on Taiwan in spring 1974.

Ellerman's Wilson Line

Ellerman's Wilson Line was, as the name so obviously suggests, part of the big Ellerman Group. Their diverse services included not only the North Sea run to Scandinavia, but further overseas to the Mediterranean and North America as well. After the *Borodino* was withdrawn in 1966, she was replaced briefly by a brand new ferry, the *Spero,* but passenger and later freighter services were eliminated entirely.

Borodino

Service Across the North Sea between Hull, Copenhagen and Aarhus. **Particulars** 3,206 gross tons; 312 × 49 × 18 ft. **Builder** Ailsa Shipbuilding Company, Troon, England, 1950. **Machinery** Steam triple expansion engines and low pressure exhaust turbine, single screw. $13\frac{1}{2}$ knots. **Capacity** 36 first class passengers. **Notes** In service 1950–66. Withdrawn December 1966 and scrapped at Ghent, Belgium.

Above *The small yacht-like* Borodino *was replaced in 1966 by a new Ellerman Wilson North Sea ferry the* Spero. *In rather quick time she was also withdrawn and passed into Greek hands* (Ellerman Wilson Line).
Top right *Having been a twin-funnel wartime transport, the* Queen of Bermuda *is the only liner with the distinction of having sailed as a one-, two- and three-stacker. She is seen here in her original form, arriving at New York* (The Port Authority of New York & New Jersey).
Centre right *Following her 1961—62 refit, the* Queen of Bermuda *has a new tapered single funnel. She is seen returning to New York for the first time with her 'new look,' in April 1962* (Furness-Bermuda Line).
Bottom right *The handsome* Ocean Monarch *was deliberately designed to resemble a large cruising yacht* (Michael Cassar).

Furness Bermuda Line

Furness Bermuda Line, an obvious arm of the giant Furness Withy Group, began service in 1919. Passenger operations with small, second-hand steamers soon prospered and led to brand new, large liners within a decade. More of a cruise operation in later years, it was discontinued in 1966, a result of increased competition and newly effected, very stringent American safety standards. Cargo operations continued for a brief time, but then these succumbed to the container transition.

Queen of Bermuda

Service Weekly six-day cruises between New York and Bermuda. Later, winter cruises from Port Everglades, Florida to the Caribbean. Occasional Atlantic crossings for overhauls in Britain. **Particulars** 22,501 gross tons; 579 × 77 × 27 ft. **Builder** Vickers Armstrong Shipbuilders Limited, Barrow-in-Furness, England, 1933. **Machinery** Steam turbo-electric, quadruple screw. Speed 20 knots. **Capacity** 733 first class passengers. **Notes** Highly popular and successful liner. Saw service as one, two and three -funnel liner. Last Furness–Bermuda liner. Launched September 1 1932. Maiden voyage March 1933. 1939–47 used as Armed Merchant Cruiser, travelling 390,000 miles and transporting 97,000 service personnel. Third 'dummy' funnel and main mast removed temporarily. Wartime capacity listed as 4,000. 1947–48 given major refit and third funnel restored. Resumed Bermuda cruises February 1949. Major refit October 1961–March 1962 at Harland & Wolff Shipyards at Belfast: new boilers fitted, new streamlined single funnel added and new raked bow increasing length to 590 ft. Tonnage re-listed as 22,552. Made final Bermuda cruise in November 1966. Sailed to Faslane, Scotland in the following month for scrapping.

Ocean Monarch

Service Weekly six-day cruises between New York and Bermuda; occasionally extended to include Nassau. Also periodic longer cruises to either Caribbean or eastern Canada. **Particulars:** 13,654 gross tons; 516 × 72 × 24 ft. **Builder** Vickers Armstrong Shipbuilders Limited, Newcastle, England, 1951. **Machinery** Steam turbines, twin screw. Speed 18 knots. **Capacity** 440 first class (later reduced to 414 first class). **Notes** Launched July 27 1950 and maiden voyage from New York on May 3 1951. Major refit 1961 and tonnage relisted as 13,581. Major refit October 1965 at Birkenhead. Withdrawn from Furness service September 1966 and laid-up in River Fal; offered for sale. Sold June 1967 to Balkanturist, Bulgarian flag. Re-named *Varna* for Mediterranean and Black Sea cruising. Used summers 1970–72 for summer St Lawrence River cruises from Montreal. 1973 summer cruises from Nice. Laid-up 1974. 1977–79 laid-up at Perama, Greece. Refitted

OCEAN MONARCH
LONDON

summer 1979 for Mediterranean cruises from Venice. Re-named *Riviera*. New service never developed. Rumoured to be chartered to World Cruise Lines for New York–Bermuda service; again never materialised. Continuous delays; continued in lay-up at Perama. Re-named *Reina Del Mar* in 1981 for Greek owners for Mediterranean and North Cape cruises; again never materialised. Destroyed by fire at Perama on May 28 1981 while undergoing repairs; later capsized. Total loss.

Furness Warren Line

The Furness Warren Line began as George Warren & Company in 1865. They were acquired by Furness Withy in 1912 and shortly thereafter the name was restyled as Furness Warren. Passenger services survived until 1961, then shifted to pure freight and finally to complete dissolution.

Nova Scotia and *Newfoundland*

Service Liverpool to Saint John's, Newfoundland, Halifax and Boston. **Particulars** 7,438/7,437 gross tons respectively; 440 × 61 × 25 ft. **Builder** Vickers-Armstrong Shipbuilders Limited, Newcastle, England, 1947 and 1948 respectively. **Machinery** Steam turbines, single screw. Speed 15 knots. **Capacity** 62 first class and 92 tourist class. **Notes** Ice-strengthened sister-ships. Commissioned September 1947 and February 1948 respectively. Both reduced to 12-passenger freighters in 1961. Sold September 1962 to Dominion Far East Line, Bahamas flag. Re-named *Francis Drake* and *George Anson* respectively for Australia–Far East–Japan service. Refitted at Glasgow with revised accommodation for 130 first class. Both scrapped spring 1971 at Kaohsiung, Taiwan.

Top left *In her original transatlantic guise the* Nova Scotia *is shown arriving at Liverpool and is being serviced by two Furness tugs* (World Ship Society Photo Library).
Bottom left *Following alterations the two former Furness ships were transferred to the Far East as the Australian-owned* Francis Drake *and* George Anson *(shown)* (World Ship Society Photo Library).
Above *The* Breconshire *and her sister-ships of the Glen Line were among the great British combination passenger-cargo liners of the post-war years* (Alex Duncan).

Glen Line

Glen Line had long had ties with the Far East. Although never quite thought of as a passenger ship company, a number of their post-World War 2 cargo liners had passenger accommodation with some 18 berths each, which was above the normal 12-passenger freighter level and which therefore required additional staff, including a ship's doctor. Merged with the Union-Castle Line in the mid-'50s, they later reduced their services to pure cargo. By 1980, however, they were no longer listed as a shipowner under the British flag.

Breconshire, Glenartney, Glenearn, Glengyle and *Glenorchy*

Service British and North European ports via Suez Canal to Malaya, Hong Kong, China and Japan; homeward include Ceylon. **Particulars** 9,061/8,992/8,960/8,957/9,324 gross tons respectively; 507 (513 for *Glenorchy*) × 66 × 30 ft. **Builder** Caledon Shipbuilding & Engineering Company, Dundee, Scotland, 1942/1940/1938/1941 respectively. **Machinery** Burmeister & Wain diesels, twin screw. Speed 17 knots. **Capacity** 18 one-class passengers. **Notes** Combination passenger-cargo ships. Diverse histories for each ship. *Breconshire* laid down for Blue Funnel Line as *Telemachus*, but completed instead as Royal Navy escort aircraft carrier HMS *Activity*. Bought by Glen Line in 1946 and rebuilt for commercial service; re-named *Breconshire*. Reduced to 12-passenger freighter status in 1964. Scrapped at Mihara, Japan in 1967.

Glenartney did war service 1940–46. Reduced to 12-passenger freighter in 1964. Scrapped in Onomichi, Japan during 1967. *Glenearn* served during World War Two as fleet supply ship, then as landing-ship. Ceased carrying passengers in 1964. Scrapped at Kaohsiung, Taiwan during early 1971.

Glengyle served during World War II as fleet supply ship, then as landing ship. Ceased carrying passengers in 1964. Sold to Ocean Steamship Company Limited, British flag in 1970 and re-named *Deucalion*. Scrapped at Kaohsiung, Taiwan during summer 1971. *Glenorchy* completed as *Priam* for Blue Funnel Line and continued as such during the war. Sold to Glen Line in 1948 and re-named *Glenorchy*. Ceased carrying passengers in 1964. Sold to Ocean Steamship Company Limited, British flag in 1970 and re-named *Phemius*. Scrapped at Kaohsiung, Taiwan in spring 1971.

Denbighshire

Service British and North European ports via Suez to Malaya, Hong Kong, China and Japan; return include Ceylon. **Particulars** 8,983 gross tons; 507 × 66 × 30 ft. **Builder** Netherlands Shipbuilding Company, Amsterdam, Holland, 1938. **Machinery** Burmeister & Wain diesels, twin screw. Speed 17 knots. **Capacity** 18 one-class passengers. **Notes** Served 1939–46 as convoy transport. Reduced to 12-passenger freighter in 1964. Sold in 1968 to China Mutual Steam Navigation Company Limited, British flag and re-named *Sarpedon*. Scrapped at Kaohsiung, Taiwan in late summer 1969.

Glengarry

Service British and North European ports via Suez Canal to Malaya, Hong Kong, China and Japan; homewards include Ceylon. **Particulars** 9,144 gross tons; 507 × 66 × 30 ft. **Builder** Burmeister & Wain Shipbuilders, Copenhagen, Denmark, 1940. **Machinery** Burmeister & Wain diesels, twin screw. Speed 17 knots. **Capacity** 18 one-class passengers. **Notes** Seized by the Germans during the invasion of Denmark. Completed as the Nazi commerce raider *Meersburg* and later re-named *Hansa*. Managed by Hamburg–American Line. Recaptured at Kiel in May 1945. Temporarily assigned to British Ministry of Transport and re-named *Empire Humber*. Later returned to Glen Line, re-named *Glengarry* and outfitted for commercial service. Ceased carrying passengers in 1964. Re-named *Dardanus* in 1970. Sold to Japanese shipbreakers in February 1971 and made final outward voyage to Far East as *Glengarry*. Scrapped at Sakaide.

Glenroy

Service British and North European ports via Suez Canal to Malaya, Hong Kong, China and Japan; homewards include Ceylon. **Particulars** 8,959 gross tons; 507 × 66 × 30 ft. **Builder** Scotts Shipbuilding & Engineering Company, Greenock, Scotland, 1938. **Machinery** Burmeister & Wain diesels, twin screw. Speed 17 knots. **Capacity** 18 one-class passengers. **Notes** Served 1940–46 first as fleet supply ship, then as landing-ship. Reduced to 12-passenger freighter in 1964. Scrapped at Onomichi, Japan in autumn 1966.

Below *The* Glenorchy *berthed along the London Docks in 1970* (Michael Cassar).
Above right *The* Denbighshire *at Genoa alongside a Mitsui-OSK freighter on June 2 1963* (Michael Cassar).
Below right *Like many Glen Line ships the* Glenroy *saw strenuous wartime service before being converted back to commercial use* (Alex Duncan).

DENBIGHSHIRE

GLENROY

Henderson Line

Henderson Line started trading as P. Henderson & Company of Glasgow, in 1840. A rival to the Bibby Line, the two companies dominated the lucrative Burmese trade. While Henderson came under Elder Dempster control in 1952, they survived as an independent name for another decade before retiring their last passenger ships and surrendering their identity.

Prome and *Salween*

Service Liverpool to Port Said, Port Sudan, Aden, Colombo and Rangoon. **Particulars** 7,043/7,063 gross tons respectively; 462 × 59 × 27 ft. **Builder** William Denny & Brothers Limited, Dumbarton, Scotland, 1937 and 1938 respectively. **Machinery** Steam turbines, single screw. Speed 14 knots. **Capacity** 76/74 first class passengers respectively. **Notes** Final Henderson Line passenger ships. Built originally with 150 passenger berths. *Prome* served 1940–45 as mine depot ship. *Salween* used as a troop-ship. Both retired in 1962. *Prome* scrapped at Bruges, Belgium and *Salween* at Hong Kong.

New Zealand Shipping Company

New Zealand Shipping Company was formed in New Zealand, at Christchurch in 1872, but with British registry. Early operations were teamed with the Shaw Savill Line, sharing the highly profitable outward migrant and then homeward meat and wool trades. New Zealand Shipping purchased the Federal Steam Navigation Company, another British shipper, in 1912, but then was itself bought by P&O four years later. The passenger division continued until 1969, and soon thereafter the remainders of the fleet were absorbed into the giant P&O Group, with the final ships being merged into P&O's *'Strath'* cargo services.

Rangitiki and *Rangitata*

Service London to Curacao, Panama Canal, Wellington and Auckland; returning via same ports, but to Southampton, then London. **Particulars** 16,985/16,969 gross tons respectively; 552 × 79 × 33 ft. **Builder** John Brown & Company Limited, Clydebank, Scotland, 1929. **Machinery** Doxford diesels, twin screw. Speed 16 knots. **Capacity** 121/123 first class and 284/288 tourist class respectively. **Notes** Ordered in 1925, but construction halted until 1927 and then completed February and October 1929 respectively. Both served 1940–47 as troop-ships with berthing for approximately 2,600 each. Major refits 1948 and 1949 respectively: new diesels, improved accommodations and increased service speeds. Sailed until 1962. *Rangitiki* sold to Spanish shipbreakers and scrapped at

The last of the Henderson Line passenger ships to Burma—the Prome **below left** *and her sister-ship the* Salween **above** (Alex Duncan).

Below *The* Rangitiki *and her sister-ship the* Rangitata *were the last twin-stackers in New Zealand Shipping's fleet* (Roger Sherlock).

RANGITANE

RUAHINE

Top left *The* Rangitane *and her sister-ship, the* Rangitoto, *were among the largest passenger-cargo combination liners ever built* (Roger Sherlock).
Centre left *The* Rangitane *in her final years, wearing the colours of the Federal Steam Navigation Company* (Michael Cassar).
Bottom left *The* Ruahine *of 1951 was the last new passenger-cargo liner to be built for New Zealand Shipping* (Roger Sherlock).
Above *The former Cunard* Parthia *was refitted and given a main mast, to become the* Remuera *for the New Zealand trade* (Roger Sherlock).

Santander during summer 1962. *Rangitata* sold to Dutch buyers and re-named *Rang*, then sold to Yugoslavian shipbreakers. Scrapped at Split in summer 1962.

Rangitoto and *Rangitane*

Service London to New Zealand via Panama (ports same as for *Rangitiki*). In later years, homeward calls at Kingston, Port Everglades and Bermuda. **Particulars** 21,809/21,867 gross tons respectively; 609 × 78 × 32 ft. **Builder** Vickers Armstrong Shipbuilders Limited, Newcastle, England, 1949 and John Brown & Company Limited, Clydebank, Scotland, 1949 respectively. **Machinery** Doxford diesels, twin screw. Speed 16½ knots. **Capacity** 436 one-class passengers. **Notes** Exceptionally large combination passenger-cargo liners Entered service August 1949 and January 1950 respectively. Main mast removed on both ships during 1965. Funnels repainted in Federal Steam Navigation Company colours in 1966. *Rangitoto* closed out 97-year-old New Zealand Shipping Company passenger service in July 1969. Sold to Oriental South America Lines (C. Y. Tung Group) and re-named *Oriental Carnaval*. Major refit: accommodation restyled as 300 first class passengers and tonnage re-listed as 19,567. Entered around-the-word cruise service from San Francisco in December 1970. Cargo hold fire on August 15 1972; damages repaired. Terminated Orient Overseas Lines' world cruise service in May 1974 and thereafter assigned to Central American and Far Eastern cruise sailings. Laid-up at Hong Kong in March 1975. Scrapped at Kaohsiung, Taiwan during spring 1976.

Rangitane withdrawn from service May 1968. Sold to Greek buyers and renamed *Jan* for single outward voyage to Kaohsiung, Taiwan scrappers. Then laid-up at Kaohsiung; scrapping delayed. Sold January 1969 to Oriental Latin America Lines (C. Y. Tung Group), re-named *Oriental Esmeralda* and fitted for world cruise service. Tonnage relisted as 19,567 and accommodation restyled as 300 first class. Liberian flag. Began world cruises June 1969. Transferred to Central American and Far Eastern cruise service in 1974. Scrapped summer 1976 at Kaohsiung, Taiwan.

Ruahine

Service London to Curacao, Panama Canal, Auckland and Wellington; return via same ports and include

Above *In her third, final career, the one-time Cunarder* Parthia *sailed as the Eastern & Australian Steamship Company's* Aramac. *Note that a dome has been added to her single funnel* (Eastern & Australian Steamship Company).
Below right *P&O-Orient liners at major British ports: the regal* Orsova *arriving at London's Tilbury Docks* **top,** *and the* Chusan *at the Southampton Docks, with the bow of the* United States *in the right foreground* **bottom** (P&O Group, Fred Rodriguez).

Tahiti, Kingston, Port Everglades and Bermuda to Southampton, then London. **Particulars** 17,851 gross tons; 584 × 75 × 29 ft. **Builder** John Brown & Company Limited, Clydebank, Scotland, 1951. **Machinery** Doxford diesels, twin screw. Speed 16½ knots. **Capacity** 267 one-class passengers. **Notes** Maiden voyage May 1951, reducing London–Wellington passage to 34 days. Main mast removed in 1965. Funnel repainted in Federal Steam Navigation Company colours in 1966. Withdrawn from service and laid-up July 1968. Sold to International Export Lines (C. Y. Tung Group), Bahamas flag, and re-named *Oriental Rio*. Later transferred to Chinese Maritime Trust (also C. Y. Tung Group), Taiwan flag. Major refit: tonnage re-listed as 17,730 and accommodation restyled as 220 first class. Began world cruise service February 1969. Scrapped at Kaohsiung, Taiwan early 1974.

Remuera

Service London to New Zealand via Panama (same ports as for *Ruahine*). **Particulars** 13,619 gross tons; 531 × 70 × 30 ft. **Builders** Harland & Wolff Limited, Belfast, Northern Ireland, 1948. **Machinery** Steam turbines, twin screw. Speed 18 knots. **Capacity** 350 one-class passengers. **Notes** Sailed for Cunard as *Parthia*, 1948–61 *(qv)*. Bought by New Zealand Shipping in November 1961 and refitted at Glasgow. Capacity increased from 250 to 350 berths. Main mast added. Entered New Zealand service June 1962. Withdrawn November 1964 and transferred to Eastern & Australian Steamship Company Limited. Re-named *Aramac* and entered Australia–Far East service February 1965. Scrapped at Kaohsiung, Taiwan spring 1970.

P&O–Orient Lines

The Orient Line was, together with P&O, the most important passenger shipper to Australia. Their sailings were almost always coordinated, seeming to be the same firm, but the most obvious difference was, of course, the naming patterns. Orient liners always used an 'O' nomenclature. Orient Line sailing ships first began service in 1820, but the firm was not fully incorporated, as the Orient Steam Navigation Company Limited, until 1878. Nearly a century later, in 1960, the more dominant P&O Company and the Orient Line were merged fully. Operations were termed as P&O–Orient Lines until 1966, when all ships, including the remaining Orient liners, reverted to the P&O name.

P&O Lines is probably, next to Cunard, the best known and most historic steamship firm in the world. It remains as the second oldest still in the same business, being surpassed by Italy's Lloyd Triestino, which dates from 1837 and is therefore two years older. Briefly called the Peninsular Steam Navigation Company (because of its initial operations to the Iberian Peninsular), the title was soon changed to the Peninsular & Oriental Steam Navigation Company, the P&O. Soon after, their operations were extended to the Eastern Mediterranean and Egypt, then to India and finally out to the Far East and Australia.

By 1960, P&O had a worldwide passenger service, using the largest liner fleet then in existence. Present-day trading has been restyled as P&O Cruises, with sailings from Britain, Australia and, using their US-based Princess Cruises, in North America. The original 'line voyages', which were once the all important mainstay of the firm, have now been reduced to a single annual trip.

Orontes

Service London to Gibraltar, Naples, Port Said, Aden, Colombo, Fremantle (and/or Adelaide), Melbourne and Sydney. Homewards include Marseilles. **Particulars** 20,186 gross tons; 664 × 75 × 30 ft. **Builder** Vickers Armstrong Shipbuilders Limited, Barrow-in-

The Oronsay *at Venice during a Mediterranean cruise* **above** *and* **below** *a night-time view of the* Canberra *at Sydney* (Both; P&O Group).

Furness, England, 1929. **Machinery** Steam turbines, twin screw. Speed 18 knots. **Capacity** 1,370 all tourist class. **Notes** The last twin-funnel P&O–Orient liner. Originally owned by Orient Line and one of five similar ships. Maiden voyage July 1929. 1939–47 used as a troop-ship. Major refit 1947–48: accommodation for 502 first class and 610 tourist class. Resumed Australian sailings June 1948. Made one-class 1953. Scrapped at Valencia, Spain in spring 1962.

Corfu and *Carthage*

Service London and/or Southampton to Port Said, Aden, Bombay, Colombo, Penang, Singapore and Hong Kong. **Particulars** 14,280 gross tons; 543 × 71 × 29 ft. **Builder** Alexander Stephen & Sons Limited, Glasgow, Scotland, 1931. **Machinery** Steam turbines, twin screw. Speed 17 knots. **Capacity** 181 first class and 213 tourist class. **Notes** Sister-ships built originally for P&O Lines. Intended to be named *Chefoo* and *Canton*. Original

Above *The* Orontes *of 1929 which retired in 1962 was the last twin-stacker in the P&O-Orient Lines fleet* (Alex Duncan).
Below *The sister-ships* Corfu *(shown) and* Carthage *maintained P&O's special service to the Far East* (Alex Duncan).

Above *The* Orion *of 1935 was considered the best decorated liner on the Australian service at the time of her maiden voyage* (P&O Group).

Below *The* Strathnaver *was originally a three-stacker but was converted with a single funnel after the Second World War* (P&O Group).

design with twin funnels and black hull colouring. Commissioned September and November 1931 respectively. Used 1939–47 as Armed Merchant Cruisers, then as transports. Resumed Far Eastern service 1949 and 1948 respectively. *Corfu* sold to Japanese breakers in August 1961 and re-named *Corfu Maru* for delivery voyage to Japan. *Carthage* sold also to Japanese scrappers and sailed to Osaka in May 1961 as *Carthage Maru.*

Orion

Service London to Australia via Suez (same ports as for *Orontes*). **Particulars** 23,696 gross tons; 665 × 82 × 30 ft. **Builder** Vickers Armstrong Shipbuilders Limited, Barrow-in-Furness, England, 1935. **Machinery** Steam turbines, twin screw. Speed 19 knots. **Capacity** Interchangeable between 706 cabin class and 700 tourist class or 1,691 all tourist class. **Notes** First major liner to be designed with only one mast. Maiden voyage August 1935. First Orient Line passenger ship to use corn-coloured hull. 1939–46 used as a troop-ship with capacity for 5,449. Rammed battleship HMS *Revenge* during Indian Ocean convoy on September 15 1941; later repaired. Major refit 1946–47. Resumed Australian sailings February 1947. 1954–55 made three Pacific voyages to North American West Coast. Used mostly as a one-class ship beginning in 1960. Chartered for use as a hotel-ship at Hamburg during summer 1963. Sold to Belgian shipbreakers in October 1963 and broken-up at Tamise.

Strathnaver

Service London to Gibraltar, Aden, occasionally Bombay, Colombo, Adelaide, Fremantle, Melbourne and Sydney. Homewards via Marseilles in addition. **Particulars** 22,270 gross tons; 664 × 80 × 29 ft. **Builder** Vickers-Armstrong Shipbuilders Limited, Barrow-in-Furness, England, 1931. **Machinery** Steam turbo-electric, twin screw. Speed 17½ knots. **Capacity** 1,252 all tourist class. **Notes** Sister-ship to *Strathaird.* Both former three-funnel design. Maiden voyage October 1931. Accommodation for 500 first class and 670 tourist class. 1939–48 used as a troop-ship. Major refit at Belfast until December 1949: two dummy funnels removed and accommodation restyled as 573 first class and 496 tourist class. Resumed Australian service January 1950. Converted to all-tourist class ship in 1954. Arrived at Hong Kong for scrapping in April 1962.

Strathaird

Service London to Australia via Suez (same ports as for *Strathnaver*). **Particulars** 22,568 gross tons; 664 × 80 × 29 ft. **Builder** Vickers-Armstrong Shipbuilders Limited, Barrow-in-Furness, England, 1932. **Machinery** Steam turbo-electric, twin screw. Speed 17½ knots.

Another of the great 'Strath' liners, the Strathaird, *also a former three-stacker, is seen leaving London for the breakers at Hong Kong* (Alex Duncan).

Capacity 1,242 all tourist class. **Notes** Sister-ship to *Strathnaver*. Former three-funnel ship. Commissioned January 1932. 1939–46 used as a transport. Rebuilt 1946–47: two dummy stacks removed and accommodation restyled as 573 first class and 496 tourist class. Resumed Australian service in January 1948. Made one-class ship in 1954. Arrived at Hong Kong in July 1961 for scrapping.

Strathmore

Service London to Australia via Suez (ports same as for *Strathnaver*). **Particulars** 23,580 gross tons; 665 × 82 × 30 ft. **Builder** Vickers-Armstrong Shipbuilders Limited, Barrow-in-Furness, England, 1935. **Machinery** Steam turbines, twin screw. Speed 19 knots. **Capacity** 497 first class and 487 tourist class. **Notes** Launched April 4 1935 by Duchess of York (later Her Majesty Queen Elizabeth, the Queen Mother). Maiden voyage to Australia October 1935. 1939–48 used as a troop-ship. Major refit 1948–49. Resumed Australian service October 1949. Made all tourist class ship with 1,080 berths in November 1961. Sold and delivered to John S. Latsis Line, Greek flag, in November 1963. Re-named *Marianna Latsi* and used as a hotel-ship in the Mediterranean and at Jeddah during Moslem pilgrim season. Used to carry pilgrims from West Africa and Libya to Jeddah during 1965. Re-named *Henrietta Latsi* during 1966. Laid-up at Eleusis, Greece in April 1967. Arrived at La Spezia, Italy in May 1969 for scrapping.

Stratheden

Service London to Gibraltar, Aden, occasionally Bombay, Colombo, Adelaide, Fremantle, Melbourne and Sydney; homewards include Marseilles. **Particulars** 23,372 gross tons; 664 × 82 × 30 ft. **Builder** Vickers-Armstrong Shipbuilders Limited, Barrow-in-Furness, England, 1937. **Machinery** Steam turbines, twin screw. Speed 19 knots. **Capacity** 527 first class and 453 tourist class. **Notes** The last of the P&O *'Strath'* liners. Launched June 10 1937 and commissioned December 1937. 1939–46 used as a troop-ship. Major refit, then resumed Australian sailings June 1947. Made four Cunard charter crossings to New York in summer 1950. Accommodation restyled as 1,200 all tourist class during 1961. Sold and delivered to John S. Latsis Line, Greek flag, in February 1964. Re-named *Henrietta Latsi* and used as a Moslem pilgrim hotel-ship in the Mediterranean and at Jeddah. Re-named *Marianna Latsi* in 1966. Scrapped at La Spezia, Italy in May 1969.

Canton

Service London and/or Southampton to Port Said, Aden, Bombay, Colombo, Penang, Singapore and Hong Kong. **Particulars** 16,033 gross tons; 563 × 73 × 29 ft. **Builder** Alexander Stephen & Sons Limited, Glasgow, Scotland, 1938. **Machinery** Steam turbines, twin screw. Speed 18 knots. **Capacity** 298 first class and 244 tourist class. **Notes** Commissioned September 1938. Originally painted with a black hull and funnel. 1939–46 served as an Armed Merchant Cruiser, then as a transport. Major refit 1946–47 and resumed Far East sailings October 1947. Arrived at Hong Kong for scrapping in October 1962.

Himalaya

Service London or Southampton to Australia via Suez (same ports as for *Stratheden*). Later used on worldwide P&O–Orient service. Also considerable

Below left *The* Strathmore *was built as a single ship entry and did not have an identical sister-ship* (Alex Duncan).
Top *An extremely rare view of the* Stratheden *at New York, during her brief charter to Cunard in the summer of 1950* (Richard K. Morse collection).
Above *The* Canton *was built as the flagship of P&O's pre-war Far Eastern passenger service* (Alex Duncan).
Below *P&O's first post-war Australian liner was the* Himalaya, *commissioned in the autumn of 1949* (Alex Duncan).

crusing, both from Britain and Australia. **Particulars** 27,955 gross tons; 709 × 91 × 31 ft. **Builder** Vickers-Armstrong Shipbuilders Limited, Barrow-in-Furness, England, 1949. **Machinery** Steam turbines, twin screw. Speed 22 knots. **Capacity** 758 first class and 401 tourist class. **Notes** Maiden voyage October 1949 and cut passage time from London to Bombay from 20 to 15 days. Used for experimental California and around-the-world sailings. Major refit 1959–60. Made one-class with 1,416 berths during 1963. Tonnage re-listed as 27,989 and later as 28,047. Arrived at Kaohsiung, Taiwan for scrapping on November 28 1974.

Orcades

Service Worldwide passenger sailings—around-the-world in both directions; to/from England to Australia and New Zealand via Suez, South Africa or Panama (and sometimes including North American Pacific Coast), to/from the Orient from North America or Australia and Circle Pacific voyages. Also cruises from London or Southampton to the Mediterranean, West Africa, the Canaries and Madeira, Northern Europe, Scandinavia and the Caribbean as well as from Australia to South Pacific ports. **Particulars** 28,396 gross tons; 709 × 90 × 30 ft. **Builder** Vickers-Armstrong Shipbuilders Limted, Barrow-in-Furness, England, 1948. **Machinery** Steam turbines, twin screw. Speed 22 knots. **Capacity** 631 first class and 734 tourist class. **Notes** Built for the Orient Line as the first of three post-war replacement liners. Launched October 14 1947 and commissioned December 1948. Cut passage time between London and Sydney from 36 to 26 days. Made first P&O–Orient liner voyage to Australia using Panama Canal route in August 1955. Major refit 1959. Converted to one-class ship with 1,635 berths in 1964. Tonnage re-listed as 28,399. Damaged in violent storm off Fremantle on June 23 1970: 28 passengers and 12 crew injured. Boiler room fire at Hong Kong on April 17 1972; repairs included replacement parts from P&O liner *Iberia*, then about to be scrapped. Laid-up at Southampton in October 1972. Arrived Kaohsiung, Taiwan on February 6 1973 for scrapping.

Oronsay

Service Worldwide passenger sailings (same outline as for *Orcades*). **Particulars** 27,632 gross tons; 709 × 90 × 30 ft. **Builder** Vickers-Armstrong Shipbuilders Limited, Barrow-in-Furness, England, 1951. **Machinery** Steam turbines, twin screw. Speed 22 knots. **Capacity** 612 first class and 804 tourist class. **Notes** Launched June 30 1950 and maiden voyage to Australia May 1951. Began P&O–Orient joint service across the Pacific to North America in January 1954. Major refit 1959. Idle at Vancouver owing to outbreak of typhoid January 14–February 4 1970. Arrived at Kaohsiung, Taiwan on October 7 1975 for scrapping. Broken-up, spring 1976.

Orsova

Service Worldwide passenger sailings (same outline as for *Orcades*). **Particulars** 28,790 gross tons; 723 × 90 ×

The Orient Line's trio of post-war Australian liners: the Orcades *of 1948* **below left;** *the* Oronsay *of 1951 on a cruise visit to Malta* **above** *and the* Orsova *of 1954* **below** *which uniquely dispensed with the conventional mast* (Michael D. J. Lennon; Michael Cassar, Roger Sherlock).

30 ft . **Builder** Vickers-Armstrong Shipbuilders Limited, Barrow-in-Furness, England, 1954. **Machinery** Steam turbines, twin screw. Speed 22 knots. **Capacity** 694 first class and 809 tourist class. **Notes** First major liner to dispense with conventional mast. Maiden voyage May 1954. Completed first P&O–Orient around-the-world sailing in July 1955. Major refit 1960. Laid-up at Southampton December 1973. Scrapped at Kaohsiung, Taiwan December 1974.

Chusan

Service Worldwide passenger sailings and consider-

Left *As if sliced open by a giant knife, the hull of the* Orsova *is opened to view at the scrapyards at Kaohsiung on Taiwan. This view has been taken directly from the aft end of the partially dismantled liner. The year is 1975* (James L. Shaw).

Below *The enormous bow of the* Orsova (P&O Group).

Above right *Although built especially for the Far Eastern passenger trade, the* Chusan *was a particularly popular cruising liner* (J. K. Byass).

Right *The last of the P&O-Orient Lines post-war rebuilding programme of liners: the* Arcadia **centre** *arriving at Colombo on her maiden voyage in March 1954, and the* Iberia **below** *arriving at New York for the first time, during a cruise in June 1959* (Both; P&O Group).

ARCADIA

able cruising (same outline as for *Orcades*). **Particulars** 24,215 gross tons; 672 × 85 × 29 ft. **Builder** Vickers-Armstrong Shipbuilders Limited, Barrow-in-Furness, England, 1950. **Machinery** Steam turbines, twin screw. Speed 22 knots. **Capacity** 475 first class and 551 tourist class. **Notes** Built for P&O Lines service to Far East and including Japan. Maiden voyage July 1950. Major refit 1959. Accommodation restyled as 464 first class and 541 tourist class. Tonnage re-listed as 24,261 gross tons. Used for cruising only beginning in 1969. Tonnage re-listed again as 24,318. Called at New York in October 1971 as part of special charter cruise from Cape Town. Sailed Southampton–Taiwan in May 1973 and then scrapped.

Arcadia

Service Worldwide passenger sailings and considerable cruising (same outline as for *Orcades*). **Particulars** 29,734 gross tons; 721 × 90 × 30 ft. **Builder** John Brown & Company Limited, Clydebank, Scotland, 1954. **Machinery** Steam turbines, twin screw. Speed 22 knots. **Capacity** 655 first class and 735 tourist class. **Notes** Launched on May 14 1953, same day as Orient Line's *Orsova (qv)*. Maiden voyage February 1954. Major refit 1959. Main mast removed 1970. Used for charter cruising from South Africa during 1971. Cruising from Australia only 1975–79. Final cruise January 1979, then sailed to Kaohsiung, Taiwan for scrapping.

Iberia

Service Worldwide passenger sailings and considerable cruising (same outline as for *Orcades*). **Particulars** 29,614 gross tons; 719 × 91 × 30 ft. **Builder** Harland & Wolff Limited, Belfast, Northern Ireland, 1954. **Machinery** Steam turbines, twin screw. Speed 22 knots. **Capacity** 673 first class and 733 tourist class. **Notes** Maiden voyage September 1954. Collision off Ceylon with tanker *Stanvac Pretoria* in March 1956. Major refit 1961. Difficult voyage in October 1969: funnel caught fire at Pago Pago, electrical failure at Honolulu, engine difficulties at Acapulco and fuel leak at Curacao. Laid-up at Southampton April 1972. Arrived Kaohsiung, Taiwan on September 5 1972 for scrapping.

Oriana

Service Worldwide passenger sailings and cruising

The unique looking Oriana *has always appeared to be a two-stacker but in fact the aft funnel device is just a ventilator—only the forward structure is a working stack* (Roger Sherlock).

A rare occasion: the two P&O-Orient giants together at Sydney. The Oriana *is unusually berthed at Woolloomooloo while the outbound* Canberra, *in the far distance to the right, has just departed Circular Quay* (P&O Group).

(same outline as for *Orcades*). Combined P&O–Orient Lines service touched at over 100 ports on five continents. **Particulars** 41,923 gross tons; 804 × 97 × 31 ft. **Builder** Vickers-Armstrong Shipbuilders Limited, Barrow-in-Furness, England, 1960. **Machinery** Steam turbines, twin screw. Speed 27½ knots. **Capacity** 638 first class and 1,496 tourist class. **Notes** Largest liner ever built in England. Fastest passenger ship ever to sail on Australian service. Launched by Princess Alexandra on November 3 1959. Maiden voyage December 1960. Cut passage time between Southampton and Sydney from four to three weeks. Boiler fire on June 17 1970, then engine room fire at Southampton on August 11 1970. Cruising only after 1973 and transferred to P&O Cruises. Tonnage relisted as 41,915 and accommodation restyled as 1,700 one-class. First transatlantic cruise to New York in August 1979. Final Australian sailing from Southampton in November 1981. Began year-round cruising from Sydney in December 1981. Capacity reduced to 1,550 in 1983. To be withdrawn in March 1986.

Canberra

Service Worldwide passenger sailings and cruising (same outline as for *Orcades*). Combined P&O–Orient Lines service touched at over 100 ports on five continents. **Particulars** 45,733 gross tons; 818 × 102 × 30 ft. **Builder** Harland & Wolff Limited, Belfast, Northern Ireland, 1961. **Machinery** Steam turbo-electric, twin screw. Speed 27½ knots. **Capacity** Adjustable from 556 first class and 1,716 tourist class or 596 first class and 1,616 tourist class. **Notes** The largest liner built at the time for a service other than the North Atlantic. P&O flagship. Launched March 16 1960 and maiden voyage June 1961. Made some voyages to New York 1962–63. Disabled by engine problems off Malta on January 5 1963; forced to return to Southampton and then Belfast for repairs. Based at New York for series of cruises February–September 1973; unsuccessful. Accommodation restyled as 1,737 one-class and transferred to P&O Cruises. Briefly laid-up at Wilmington, North Carolina in February–March 1973. Aground off Grenada July 12–15 1973, then off St

Above *The* Canberra *at anchor off Gibraltar during a cruise* (Michael D. J. Lennon).

Below *The* Canberra*'s triumphant return to Southampton following her exceptional duty in the South Atlantic, July 11 1982* (Southern Newspapers Ltd).

Above *During the* Canberra*'s maiden visit to Yokohama, Japan, on March 15 1966, she was berthed just behind another P&O liner, the* Chitral. *On the north side of the same terminal is the* George Anson *of the Dominion Far East Line and the* Sagafjord *of the Norwegian America Line* (P&O Group).

Below *The* Canberra *at Madeira* (P&O Group).

Thomas on August 14. Cruising from Southampton only beginning in October 1973. Later, winter cruises from Sydney as well. Requisitioned by British government in April 1982 for use as a troop-ship to the Falkland Islands. Departed from Southampton on April 8, bound for South Atlantic. Also used as a hospital ship. Released in July and then refitted; Resumed cruising.

Chitral and *Cathay*

Service London, Rotterdam and Southampton to Port Said, Aden, Colombo, Penang, Port Swettenham, Singapore, Hong Kong, Yokohama and Kobe. Homewards via Singapore, Port Swettenham, Penang, Colombo, Aden, Port Said, Naples and Le Havre to London. **Particulars** 13,821/13,809 gross tons respectively; 558 × 70 × 28 ft. **Builders** Chantiers de L'Atlantique, St. Nazaire, France, 1956 and Cockerill-

Left Canberra *departs from Lisbon* (Luis Miguel Correia).
Below *P&O's last speciality combination passenger-cargo liners the* Chitral *(shown) and her sister-ship the* Cathay, *were retired in 1969* (Richard K. Morse collection).
Right *The final arrival of P&O's* Cathay *at the Southampton Docks in the autumn of 1969* (P&O Group).

CATHAY

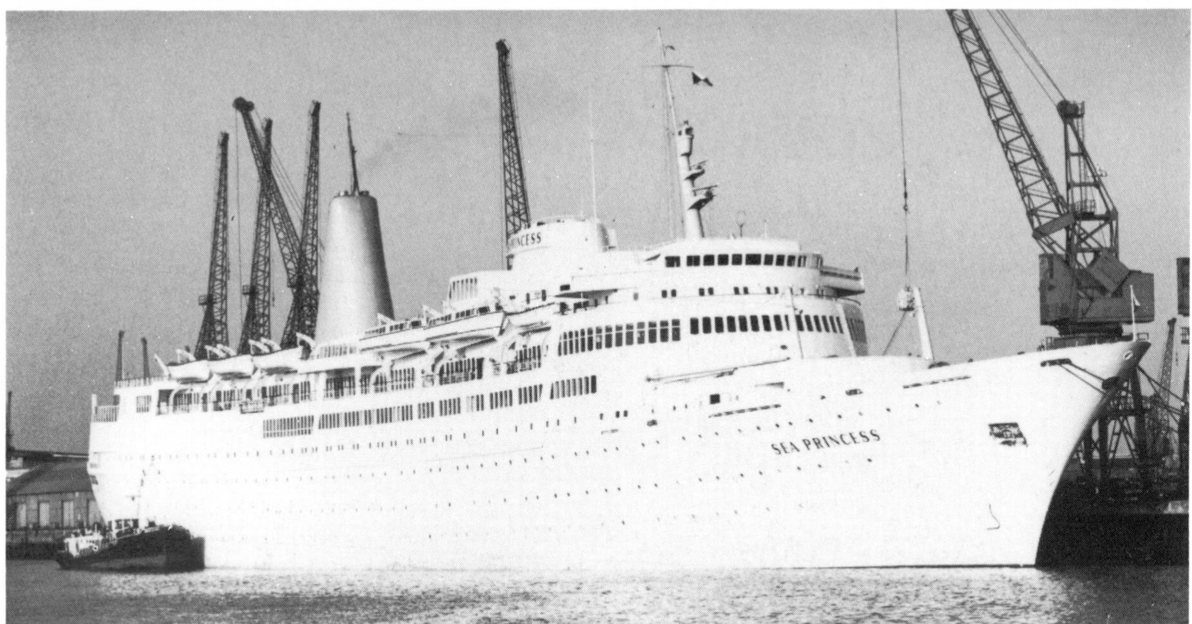

Ougree Shipyard, Hoboken, Belgium, 1957 respectively. **Machinery** Steam turbines, twin screw. Speed 16½ knots. **Capacity** 240 first class. **Notes** Sister-ships built originally for Belgian Line Antwerp–Congo service as *Jadotville* and *Baudouinville* respectively. Sold to P&O in January 1961. Refitted for Far Eastern passenger-cargo service. *Chitral* rumoured to become hotel-ship, then freighter in 1969. Used April–October 1970 for series of Mediterranean cruises from Genoa; highly unsuccessful. Sold December 1970 to Eastern & Australian Steamship Company and transferred to Australia–Far East service. Sold to Taiwan breakers in December 1975; scrapped during summer 1976 at Kaohsiung.

Cathay transferred to Eastern & Australian Steamship Company in November 1969 and transferred to Australia–Far East service. Reportedly sold to Nan Yang Shipping Company of Macau in 1975 for use as training ship, then promptly resold to China Ocean Shipping Company, People's Republic of China. Re-

Top far left *Sweden's* Kungsholm *as seen prior to her purchase by P&O Cruises* (Roger Sherlock).
Bottom far left Kungsholm, *with her forward dummy funnel removed and considerably altered, became the P&O Cruises'* Sea Princess (Michael D. J. Lennon).
Above *An unusual meeting: the coincidental rendezvous of the* Canberra *and* Sea Princess *at the Hong Kong Ocean Terminal in March 1982* (P&O Group).
Left *Photographed at Lisbon, the stern section of* Sea Princess (Luis Miguel Correia).

named *Kengshin*, then *Shanghai*. Still in Chinese service.

Sea Princess

Service 1979–82: Cruising from Sydney to Pacific ports. Thereafter, transferred to Southampton cruising: Mediterranean, West Africa, Caribbean, Scandinavia, etc. Also cruises from Mediterranean ports. **Particulars** 27,670 gross tons; 660 × 86 × 26 ft. **Builder** John Brown & Company Limited, Clydebank, Scotland, 1966. **Machinery** Gotaverken diesels, twin screw. Speed 21 knots. **Capacity** 750 first class. **Notes** Sailed 1966–75 for Swedish American Line, Swedish flag as *Kungsholm,* mostly on long-distance cruises from New York. Sold December 1975 to Flagship Cruises, Liberian flag; continued cruising under Swedish name. Sold to Sea Leasing Corporation, British flag, in September 1978 and leased to P&O. Re-named *Sea Princess* and major refit at Bremen. Entered P&O Cruises service in January 1979.

The last of Pacific Steam Navigation's passenger liners, the Reina Del Mar, *which sailed for just over seven years to South America (1956–63)* (Roger Sherlock).

Pacific Steam Navigation Company

The Pacific Steam Navigation Company was actually first created by an American, who served in Chile as a merchant shipper. He secured a British government charter in 1839 for services along the West Coast of South America. A run to England began in 1868, using the Strait of Magellan route until the Panama Canal opened in 1914. The firm was bought out by the Royal Mail Lines in 1938, and later worked into the parent Furness Withy Group. Passenger service ended in 1963 but cargo services continue at the time of writing.

Reina Del Mar

Service Liverpool to La Rochelle, Santander, Coruna, Bermuda, Nassau, Havana, Kingston, La Guaira, Curacao, Cartagena, Cristobal, La Libertad, Callao, Arica, Antofagasta and Valparaiso. Homewards via same ports and also Vigo and Plymouth. **Particulars** 20,334 gross tons; 601 × 78 × 30 ft. **Builder** Harland & Wolff Limited, Belfast, Northern Ireland, 1956. **Machinery** Steam turbines, twin screw. Speed 18 knots. **Capacity** 207 first class, 216 cabin class and 343 tourist class. **Notes** Last Pacific Steam Navigation liner. Launched June 7 1955 and maiden voyage May 1956. Considerable cruising 1963–64. Rumoured to be sold to Greek Chandris Group in January 1964; never materialised. Withdrawn from South American service March 1964 and given 13-week refit at Belfast for year-round cruising. Accommodation restyled as 1,047 one-class and tonnage re-listed as 21,501. Commenced charter to Travel Savings Limited with Union-Castle management in June 1964. Repainted in Union-Castle colours in November 1964. Full operation by Union-Castle thereafter *(qv)*.

Princess Cruises

Princess Cruises was formed in the mid-'60s by Seattle interests, who innovatively saw a bright future in winter-time Mexican cruising from California. Seasonal operations began with the chartered *Princess Patricia,* which was normally on the summer Alaska run for Canadian Pacific. Cruising soon expanded, with Princess using fulltime chartered tonnage, to Alaska, the trans-Panama route and into the Caribbean. This firm was acquired by the P&O Group in 1974 and thereafter became a British-flag venture.

Above *When brand new, the* Spirit of London *had a maiden cruise from Southampton to the Caribbean islands. She is shown at Southampton Docks, berthed just behind the* Orsova (P&O Group).
Below *Re-named as the* Sun Princess *the same liner is seen in a poetic view at San Juan, Puerto Rico* (Princess Cruises).

Spirit of London/Sun Princess

Service Summer cruises from Vancouver to Alaska; winters from San Juan to the Caribbean. Also trans-Panama Canal cruises. **Particulars** 17,370 gross tons; 535 ×75 ×21 ft. **Builder** Cantieri Riuniti del Tirreno e Riuniti Spa Shipyard, Genoa, Italy, 1972. **Machinery** Fiat diesels, twin screw. Speed 20 knots. **Capacity** 742 cruise passengers (862 maximum berths). **Notes** Originally ordered by Norwegian Caribbean Lines, Norwegian flag, as *Seaward* for Florida–Caribbean service. Then bought in early stages of construction by P&O Lines, later parent to Princess Cruises. Completed November 1972 as *Spirit of London*. Commenced North American cruising January 1973. Transferred to Princess Cruises in October 1974 and re-named as *Sun Princess*. Began winter cruises from San Juan in January 1977.

Pacific Princess

Service Four-week cruises from Los Angeles to Mexico, Panama Canal, the Caribbean and return; seven to 14-day cruises from Los Angeles to Mexico; seven to 14-day summer cruises from San Francisco or Vancouver to Alaska; occasional long cruises from California to the South Pacific. **Particulars** 19,904 gross tons; 550 × 80 × 20 ft. **Builder** Nordseewerke Shipyard, Rheinstahl, West Germany, 1971. **Machinery** Fiat diesels, twin screw. Speed 20 knots. **Capacity** 646 cruise passengers (750 maximum berths). **Notes** Sister-ship to *Island Princess*. Launched May 9 1970 and commissioned as *Sea Venture* In May 1971 for Flagship Cruises, Norwegian flag. Used for cruises from New York to Bermuda and the Caribbean. Sold to P&O (Princess Cruises) in October 1974 and delivered in April 1975. Re-named *Pacific Princess* and transferred to British flag. Began use as a floating prop for US television series 'Love Boat' in 1976.

Island Princess

Service North American cruising (same outline as for *Pacific Princess*). **Particulars** 19,907 gross tons; 550 × 80 × 20 ft. **Builder** Nordseewerke Shipyard, Rheinstahl, West Germany, 1972. **Machinery** Fiat diesels, twin screw. Speed 20 knots. **Capacity** 646 cruise passengers (750 maximum berths). **Notes** Launched March 6 1971 as *Island Venture* and delivered to Flagship Cruises, Norwegian flag, in January 1972. Commenced American cruise sailings, mostly from New York to Bermuda and the Caribbean. Sold in

Below left *The* Pacific Princess*—US television's well known 'Love Boat'—passing under the Lion's Gate Bridge at Vancouver* (Roger Sherlock).
Above *The cruise-ship* Island Princess *was the former Norwegian* Island Venture, *bought by P&O-Princess in late 1974* (Roger Sherlock).
Below *The most expensive P&O liner of all time, the* Royal Princess, *commissioned in the autumn of 1984* (P&O Group).

December 1974 to P&O–Princess Cruises and renamed *Island Princess.* Transferred to British flag.

Royal Princess

Service North American cruising—similar outline to *Pacific Princess.* **Particulars** 44,348 gross tons, 761 × 96 × 21 ft. **Builder** Wartsila Shipyard, Helsinki, Finland, 1984. **Machinery** Wartsila Pielstick diesels, twin screw. Speed 22 knots. **Capacity** 1,260 cruise passengers. **Notes** Named November 15 1984 by HRH the Princess of Wales in Southampton's Western Dock. Sailed November 19 1984 for maiden voyage to Miami prior to cruise through Panama Canal to commence service on the US West Coast.

Royal Mail Lines

Royal Mail Lines dates from 1840 when, as the Royal Mail Steam Packet Company, it ran services to the West Indies. These were later expanded to include the East Coast of South America, which became far more important and profitable, due to the southward immigrant trade from Spain and Portugal, and from the northbound meat going to Britain from the Argentine. Liner service to South America, using the last established three-class ships under the British flag, survived until 1969. Luxury, one-class cruising aboard the *Andes*, the company's last passenger liner, continued for two years further. Presently, the company's interests are in the freight trades only.

Andes

Service Cruising from Southampton to the North Cape, Baltic, Mediterranean, West Africa, the Canaries, Caribbean and periodic long-distance cruises to South Africa, South America and the United States. **Particulars** 26,860 gross tons; 669 × 83 × 29 ft. **Builder** Harland & Wolff Limited, Belfast, Northern Ireland, 1939. **Machinery** Steam turbines, twin screw. Speed 21 knots. **Capacity** 500 first class. **Notes** Royal Mail Lines flagship. Launched March 7 1939. Maiden voyage set for September 1939 cancelled owing to outbreak of war. Outfitted instead as a trooper with wartime capacity of 4,096. Made fastest round-the-world passage to date in 1940: 72 days from Liverpool to Panama, Wellington, Karachi, Suez and return to Liverpool. Major refit 1947–48: restored for commercial service with 324 first class and 204 cabin class berths. Maiden voyage January 1948 from Southampton to East Coast of South America. Converted 1959–60

Below left *One of the finest cruise-ships of all time, the* Andes *had a devoted club-like following that included many millionaires* (Vincent Messina collection).
This page *Two of the three final Royal Mail liners built for the South American trade; the* Amazon **above** *and the* Aragon **below** (Royal Mail Lines; Roger Sherlock).

to full-time cruise-ship. Engine trouble during final cruise February 1971. Arrived at Ghent, Belgium in May 1971 for scrapping.

Amazon, Aragon and *Arlanza*

Service London to Cherbourg, Vigo, Lisbon, Las Palmas, Rio de Janeiro, Santos, Montevideo and Buenos Aires. Homewards call at Boulogne instead of Cherbourg. **Particulars** 20,348/20,362/20,362 gross tons respec-tively, 584 × 78 × 28 ft. **Builder** Harland & Wolff Limited, Belfast, Northern Ireland, 1959/1960/-1960 respectively. **Machinery** Harland & Wolff turbo-charged diesels, twin screw. Speed 17½ knots. **Capacity** 92 first class, 82 cabin class (15 first class and 30 cabin class were interchangeable) and 275 third class. **Notes** Three sister-ships that were last ships built to carry third class and the last group with three classes. *Amazon* was first of the trio and commissioned in January 1960. All sold to Shaw Savill Line in 1968–69 and re-named *Akaroa, Aranda* and *Arawa* respectively *(qv). Aragon* closed out Royal Mail's South American passenger service in February 1969.

Shaw Savill Line

The Shaw Savill Line was organised by two pioneer shippers, Robert Shaw and Walter Savill. Scheduled operations began in 1882, with particular emphasis (and profit) coming from the Australia–New Zealand migrants and then the homeward cargos of meat and wool. Their final passenger ships were, in fact, without any cargo spaces at all. Used in the very final years as cruise-ships, they abandoned passenger service entirely by 1976.

Dominion Monarch

Service London and Southampton to Las Palmas, Cape Town, Fremantle, Melbourne, Sydney, Wellington and return, three-month round-trips. **Particulars** 26,463 gross tons; 682 × 85 × 34 ft. **Builder** Swan, Hunter & Wigham Richardson Limited, Newcastle, England, 1939. **Machinery** Doxford diesels, quadruple screw. Speed 19½ knots. **Capacity** 508 first class. **Notes** Shaw Savill's largest liner and flagship. Launched July 27 1938. Commissioned February 1939. Made record passage from London to Fremantle in 23 days, 17 hours. Began war service as a transport in August 1940 with listed capacity of 3,663. Major refit 1947–48 and restored for commercial service. Resumed sailings December 1948. Sold to Japanese scrappers in February 1962, then briefly used as hotel-ship at Seattle during summer 1962. Departed Seattle in November 1962 as *Dominion Monarch Maru* bound for scrapping at Osaka.

Below *The beautifully decorated* Dominion Monarch *was built especially for all-first class passenger service to Australia and New Zealand* (Roger Sherlock).

Top right *The* Corinthic *was one of a special Shaw Savill quartet to be built with very fine first class accommodation for 85 passengers as well as considerable refrigerated cargo space for British-bound meats.* (Alex Duncan).

Right *The* Gothic—*specially painted in white—arriving at Valletta, Malta on May 4 1954 while serving as a royal yacht* (Michael Cassar).

Corinthic, Athenic, Gothic **and** ***Ceramic***

Service London to Curacao, Panama Canal, Auckland and Wellington; returning via same ports. **Particulars** 15,682/15,187/15,911/15,896 gross tons respectively; 560 × 71 × 29 ft. **Builders** Cammell Laird & Company, Birkenhead, England, 1947; Harland & Wolff Limited, Belfast, Northern Ireland, 1947; Swan Hunter & Wigham Richardson Limited, Newcastle, England, 1948; and Cammell Laird & Company, Birkenhead, England, 1948 respectively. **Machinery** Steam turbines, twin screw. Speed 17 knots. **Capacity** 85 first class only. Four sister-ships. *Corinthic* first of class launched May 30th 1946 and commissioned April 1947. *Corinthic* and *Athenic* both ceased carrying passengers in spring 1965. Thereafter used as freighters. Both arrived at Taiwan in October 1969 for scrapping.

Gothic refitted in 1951 for use as royal yacht for Commonwealth Tour by King George VI and Queen Elizabeth. Voyage cancelled owing to King's declining health and subsequent death. Selected again in October 1953 for Queen Elizabeth's II's Commonwealth Tour, October 1953–May 1954. Repainted in white for the occasion. Carried the Queen, Duke of Edinburgh and their party to New Zealand, Australia, Ceylon. The Queen left ship in East Africa. Thereafter *Gothic* resumed normal sailings. Seriously damaged by fire on August 2 1968 while some 800 miles from Wellington and seven people killed. Reached Wellington on August 6 and given temporary repairs. Reached Liverpool October 10 and full repairs thought to be uneconomic. Arrived Kaohsiung, Taiwan on August 13 1969 for scrapping.

Ceramic broken-up at Tamise, Belgium in summer 1972.

Southern Cross

Service Around-the-world sailings—approximate 76-day round voyages from Southampton to Bermuda, sometimes Port Everglades, Trinidad, Curacao, Panama Canal, Tahiti, Fiji, Wellington, Auckland, Sydney, Melbourne, Fremantle, Durban, Cape Town, Las Palmas and return to Southampton. **Particulars** 20,204 gross tons; 604 × 78 × 25 ft. **Builder** Harland & Wolff Limited, Belfast, Northern Ireland, 1955. **Machinery** Steam turbines, twin screw. Speed 20 knots. **Capacity** 1,100 tourist class. **Notes** First major liner with engines and funnel placed so far aft. Launched by Queen Elizabeth II on August 17 1954. Commissioned March 1955 with alternating east- and west-about world voyages. Withdrawn from service March 1971 and laid-up at Southampton. Moved to River Fal in April 1972. Rumoured to become floating hotel and recreation centre on Cornwall coast; never materialised. Sold to Ulysses Line, Greek flag, in March 1973. Re-named *Calypso*. Refitted 1973–75. Entered cruise service June 1975. Transferred to Western Cruise Lines, Panama flag, in September 1980 and re-named *Azure Seas*. Exceptionally high purchase price of $23 million. Entered Los Angeles–Mexico cruise run in November 1980.

Northern Star

Service Around-the-world sailings—four-month voyages alternating with *Southern Cross:* Southampton to Las Palmas, Cape Town, Durban, Fremantle, Melbourne, Sydney, Wellington or Auckland, Fiji, Tahiti, Panama Canal, Curacao, Trinidad and return to Southampton. Occasional calls at Acapulco, Barbados and Lisbon. **Particulars** 24,731 gross tons; 650 × 83 × 26 ft. **Builder** Vickers-Armstrong Shipbuilders Limited Newcastle, England, 1962. **Machinery** Steam turbines, twin screw, Speed 20 knots. **Capacity** 1,437 tourist class. **Notes** Launched by Her Majesty Queen Elizabeth, the Queen Mother on June 27 1961. Commissioned July

Below *The* Southern Cross *of 1954 was the first major liner to have her funnel and engines placed so far aft* (Michael D. J. Lennon).
Top right *The* Northern Star *was a modified and slightly larger version of the highly successful* Southern Cross—*she is shown here in her original Shaw Savill colours* (Roger Sherlock).
Right *In her later years, amongst other changes, the* Northern Star *was given new funnel colours. Here she is arriving at Lisbon during a cruise* (Luis Miguel Correia).
Bottom right *Royal Mail's former* Amazon *dressed in Shaw Savill livery and re-named* Akaroa (Roger Sherlock).

1962. Tonnage re-listed in 1968 as 23,983. After 1971, increased use as a cruise-ship. Engine room explosion off Venice on June 12 1974. Further mechanical problems in November 1974. Withdrawn from service in October 1975; continuous mechanical difficulties. Scrapped at Kaohsiung, Taiwan in spring 1976.

Akaroa, Aranda and *Arawa*

Service Mostly around-the-world sailings—London to the Azores, Barbados, Trinidad, Curacao, Panama Canal, Tahiti, Auckland, Wellington, Sydney, Melbourne, Fremantle, Durban, Cape Town, Las Palmas and return to London. Some voyages in reverse direction and ports sometimes varied. Occasional cruises from Sydney and Auckland. **Particulars** 20,348/ 20,362/ 20,362 gross tons respectively, 584 × 78 × 28 ft. **Builder** Harland & Wolff Limited, Belfast, Northern Ireland, 1959/1960/1960 respectively. **Machinery** Harland & Wolff turbo-charged diesels, twin screw. Speed 17½ knots. **Capacity** 470 one-class. **Notes** Formerly *Amazon, Aragon* and *Arlanza* respectively of Royal Mail Lines *(qv)* . Transferred to Shaw Savill in 1968–69. *Akaroa* made first sailing in May 1968. Later, same ship seriously damaged by fire on April 15 1970 while 1,000 miles south-west of the Azores. Returned to Britain and repaired. In April 1971 rumoured to become a floating hotel in the Seychelles. Soon afterward, sold to Uglands Rederi, Norwegian flag, for conversion to auto carrier with a capacity of 3,000 cars. Re-named *Akarita.* Converted at Grimstad, Norway and then completed at Rijeka, Yugoslavia. Tonnage re-listed as 11,081. Worldwide service. Sold 1978 to Sagitta Liberia Limited, Liberian flag, and re-named *Hual Akarita.* Sold to Ace Autoline Line, Liberian flag, in 1981 and reverted to *Akarita.* Sold for scrapping in Taiwan in December 1981.

Aranda and *Arawa* sold to Leif Höegh, Norwegian flag, in 1971 and converted to car carriers at Rijeka, Yugoslavia. Tonnages re-listed as 10,665. Capacity 3,000 autos each. Re-named *Höegh Traveller* and *Höegh Transit* respectively. A year later, in 1972, *Höegh Transit* re-named *Höegh Trotter.* Both sold in 1978 to Ace Navigation Company, Liberian flag, and re-named *Hual Traveller* and *Hual Trotter* respectively. Then, in June 1981, both re-named again as *Traveller* and *Trotter.* Sold to Taiwan scrappers in autumn 1981 and broken-up at Kaohsiung.

Ocean Monarch

Service Mostly cruising—either from British ports or from Sydney. Occasional line voyages between Britain and Australia. **Particulars** 25,971 gross tons; 640 × 85

Left *The* Aragon, *which became the* Aranda, *is seen as the totally rebuilt auto carrier* Höegh Traveller (Michael Cassar).
Above *The original* Arlanza *became the* Arawa *for Shaw Savill and then the cargo carrier* Höegh Transit *then* Höegh Trotter, Hual Trotter *and finally the* Trotter *before being scrapped on Taiwan in late 1981* (Michael Cassar).
Below *Possibly Shaw Savill's least successful liner, the* Ocean Monarch, *the former* Empress of England, *in 1970* (Roger Sherlock).

× 29 ft. **Builder** Vickers-Armstrong Shipbuilders ers Limited, Newcastle-upon-Tyne, England, 1957. **Machinery** Steam turbines, twin screw. Speed 20 knots. **Capacity** 1,372 one-class passengers. **Notes** Sailed as *Empress of England* for Canadian Pacific 1957–70 *(qv)*. Bought by Shaw Savill in February 1970. Maiden voyage from Liverpool to Australia in April 1970. Major but delayed refit September 1970–October 1971. Entered cruise service from Southampton October 1971. Frequent mechanical problems in autumn 1974. Uneconomic to repair. Sold to Taiwan scrappers in summer 1975.

Union-Castle Line

The Union Castle Line was long the best known passenger firm in the African trades, its position being quite similar to that held by Cunard on the North Atlantic and by P&O to regions east of the Suez. However, their creation was far more recent, coming about in 1900 when the rival Union Steam Company and the Castle Mail Packet Company were merged. Passenger schedules were based on two separate routes, 'the Cape Mail Express' to South Africa and then the round-Africa service, sailing completely around that continent either eastabout or westabout. Noticeable cutbacks in passenger service did not begin until the mid-'60s. The final Cape Town mail liners continued until 1977. While the distant remains of Union-Castle are in cargo and charter shipping, those same African routes are now plied by giant container-ships.

Carnarvon Castle

Service Mailship run from Southampton to Madeira or Las Palmas, Cape Town, Port Elizabeth, East London and Durban. **Particulars** 20,148 gross tons; 686 × 73 × 32 ft. **Builder** Harland & Wolff Limited, Belfast, Northern Ireland, 1926. **Machinery** Burmeister & Wain diesels, twin screw. Speed 20 knots. **Machinery** 134 first class and 450 tourist class. **Notes** First Union-Castle motorliner and first ship to exceed 20,000 tons. Entered service June 1926. Major refit 1937–38: original twin squat funnels replaced by one single stack, more powerful diesels fitted and lengthened. Record passage in 1938 from Southampton to Cape Town in 12 days, 13 hours; record stood until 1954. 1939–47 sailed as an Armed Merchant Cruiser, then as a troop-ship. Damaged Nazi raider *Thor* off South America in December 1940. 1947–49 sailed on immigrant service to South Africa. 1949–50 major refit and restored for commercial service. Scrapped in Japan autumn 1962.

Winchester Castle

Service Mailship run to South Africa (same ports as for *Carnarvon Castle*). **Particulars** 20,001 gross tons; 657 × 75 × 32 ft. **Builder** Harland & Wolff Limited, Belfast, Northern Ireland, 1930. **Machinery** Burmeister & Wain diesels, twin screw. Speed 20 knots. **Capacity** 189 first class and 398 tourist class. **Notes** Maiden voyage October 1930. Rebuilt 1938: twin squat funnels replaced by single stack and more powerful diesels fitted. 1940–47 used for war service. 1947–48

Below left *An aerial view of the Southampton Docks in December 1963: in the forground, berthed at the Ocean Terminal, is the* Queen Mary; *while in the more distant Western Docks are (***from left to right***) the* Empress of Britain, Canberra, Pendennis Castle, Pretoria Castle *and* Stirling Castle (Port of Southampton Commission).
Above *The* Carnarvon Castle *was built with two squat stacks but re-engined and refitted in the '30s, she was given a large single stack in a design arrangement that became common to Union-Castle liners* (Richard K. Morse collection).
Below *An enormous collection of British liners during the devastating seamen's strike of May—June 1966. There are eight Union-Castle liners alone: the* Windsor Castle, S. A. Vaal, Edinburgh Castle, Reina Del Mar, Good Hope Castle, Pendennis Castle, S. A. Oranje *and* Capetown Castle (Port of Southampton Commission).

immigrant service to South Africa. 1948 given major refit for return to commercial service. Scrapped at Mihara, Japan in late 1960.

Stirling Castle and *Athlone Castle*

Service Mailship run from Southampton via Madeira or Las Palmas to Cape Town, Port Elizabeth, East London and Durban. **Particulars** 25,554/25,567 gross tons respectively; 725 × 82 × 32 ft. **Builder** Harland & Wolff Limited, Belfast, Northern Ireland, 1936. **Machinery** Burmeister & Wain diesels, twin screw. Speed 20 knots. **Capacity** 245 first class and 538 tourist class. **Notes** Sister-ships. Used as troop-ships 1939–46. Refitted 1946–47 for resumption of commercial service. *Stirling Castle* scrapped at Mihara, Japan in spring 1966 and *Athlone Castle* at Kaohsiung, Taiwan in autumn 1965.

Capetown Castle

Service Mailship run to South Africa (same ports as for *Stirling Castle*). **Particulars** 27,002 gross tons; 734 × 82 × 32 ft. **Builder** Harland & Wolff Limited, Belfast, Northern Ireland, 1938. **Machinery** Burmeister & Wain diesels, twin screw. Speed 20 knots. **Capacity** 243 first class and 553 tourist class. **Notes** Longest motor-liner ever built. Launched September 23 1937 and commissioned April 1938. Troop-ship 1939–46. Major refit in 1946 and resumed commercial service in January 1947. Engine room explosion off Las Palmas on October 17 1960; seven killed. Made one-class in 1965. Scrapped at La Spezia, Italy in autumn 1967.

Durban Castle and *Warwick Castle*

Service Around Africa—London and Rotterdam to Las Palmas, Ascension, St Helena, Walvis Bay, Cape Town, Port Elizabeth, Durban, Lourenco Marques, Beira, Dar-es-Salaam, Zanzibar, Tanga, Mombasa, Aden, Suez, Port Said, Genoa, Marseilles, Gibraltar and return to London. Some sailings in reverse direction. **Particulars** 17,382/17,387 gross tons; 595 × 76 × 29 ft. **Builder** Harland & Wolff Limited, Belfast, Northern Ireland, 1938 and 1939 respectively. **Machinery** Burmeister & Wain diesels, twin screw. Speed 18½ knots. **Capacity** 180 first class and 359 tourist class. **Notes** Sister-ships. *Warwick Castle* completed as *Pretoria Castle* and renamed in 1946. 1939–46 war service. *Warwick Castle* bought by Royal Navy in 1942 and rebuilt as an aircraft carrier. Re-purchased by Union-Castle in 1946 and then rebuilt as a passenger ship. Both used on the Mailship express run 1947–50, then resumed around Africa sailings. *Durban Castle* scrapped at Hamburg in spring 1962; *Warwick Castle* broken-up at Barcelona in summer 1962.

Left *The* Winchester Castle *was the only Union-Castle mail-ship to retain her original straight stem* (Roger Sherlock).
Two highly successful Union-Castle sister-ships—the Stirling Castle **above** *seen here at Cape Town and her identical sister-ship the* Althone Castle **below** *seen at Southampton* (Alex Duncan; Union-Castle).
Bottom *For many years the* Capetown Castle *of 1938 was the longest motor-liner afloat* (Union Castle).

Above *The* Pretoria Castle *of 1938 which became the* Warwick Castle *in 1946 and her sister-ship were smaller versions of the Cape Town mail-ships. This ship was gutted and turned into an aircraft carrier during the Second World War but converted back to a passenger ship in 1946—47* (Alex Duncan).
When commissioned in 1948, the Edinburgh Castle **below** *and her sister-ship, the* Pretoria Castle **above right**, *were the largest liners of the Union-Castle fleet and the most luxurious ships in African service. In 1962, both ships were refitted, their forward masts stumped and aft masts removed completely. In 1966, the* Pretoria Castle *was transferred to the South African Marine Corporation, painted in their colours and re-named* S. A. Oranje (Union Castle; World Ship Society Photo Library).
Below right *The* Braemar Castle, *as built, with a flat-topped funnel* (Alex Duncan).

Pretoria Castle/S. A. Oranje and *Edinburgh Castle*

Service Mailship express run—Southampton via Madeira or Las Palmas to Cape Town, Port Elizabeth, East London and Durban. **Particulars** 28,705 gross tons; 747 × 84 × 32 ft. **Builder** Harland & Wolff Limited, Belfast, Northern Ireland, 1948. **Machinery** Steam turbines, twin screw. Speed 22 knots. **Capacity** 214 first class and 541 tourist class. **Notes** Sister-ships. *Edinburgh Castle* launched by Princess Margaret. Commissioned July and December 1948 respectively. Main mast removed aboard both ships 1962. Accommodation restyled in 1964 as 154 first class and 491 tourist class. *Pretoria Castle* transferred to operation of South African Marine Corporation (Safmarine Lines) in February 1966 and re-named *S. A. Oranje.*

Transferred to South African flag in March 1969. Withdrawn October 1975 and sold to Taiwan scrappers. *Edinburgh Castle* withdrawn April 1976. Reportedly sold to Far Eastern buyers for further trading, but failed to materialise. Scrapped during summer 1976 at Kaohsiung, Taiwan.

Rhodesia Castle, Kenya Castle and *Braemar Castle*

Service Around Africa—from London and Rotterdam to Las Palmas, Ascension, St Helena, Walvis Bay, Cape Town, Port Elizabeth, Durban, Lourenco Marques, Beira, Dar-es-Salaam, Zanzibar, Tanga, Mombasa, Aden, Suez, Port Said, Genoa, Marseilles, Gibraltar and return to London. Some voyages in reverse direction. **Particulars** 17,041/17,041/17,029 gross tons respectively; 576 × 74 × 28 ft. **Builder** Harland & Wolff Limited, Belfast, Northern Ireland, 1951/1952/1952 respectively. **Machinery** Steam turbines, twin screw. Speed 17½ knots. **Capacity** 552/526/552 cabin class respectively. **Notes** Three sister-ships. *Rhodesia Castle* as first of trio was commissioned in November 1951. All given major refits 1960–61: domed funnels and accommodation restyled as 446/446/453 cabin class respectively. *Rhodesia Castle* and *Kenya Castle* assigned to revised service in April 1962 to East African ports only, terminating at Durban and return. *Rhodesia Castle* laid-up May 1967. Arrived Kaohsiung, Taiwan in October 1967 for scrapping.

Kenya Castle laid-up April 1967 and later sold to Chandris Group, Greek flag. Re-named *Amerikanis*. Rebuilt at Piraeus for North American cruise service

Above *Following major refits in 1961—62 the* Rhodesia Castle *and her two sisters appeared with domed funnels* (Roger Sherlock).
Above right *The* Reina Del Mar *under Union-Castle management was a highly popular cruise-ship sailing from both British and South African ports* (Alex Duncan).

with 910 first class berths. Tonnage re-listed as 19,337. Entered service August 1968. Still in service.

Braemar Castle rumoured to become cruise-ship for Union-Castle in 1965; never materialised. Sold to breakers in November 1965 and scrapped at Faslane, Scotland.

Reina Del Mar

Service Cruising, both from Southampton and Cape Town. **Particulars** 21,501 gross tons; 601 × 78 × 30 ft. **Builder** Harland & Wolff Limited, Belfast, Northern Ireland, 1956. **Machinery** Steam turbines, twin screw. Speed 18 knots. **Capacity** 998 cruise berths (1,026 maximum berths). **Notes** Sailed for Pacific Steam Navigation as *Reina Del Mar* on South American route *(qv)*. Commenced 13-week refit in March 1964 so as to be more suitable for cruising. Commenced charter to Travel Savings Limited with management by Union-Castle in June 1964. Repainted in Union-Castle colours in November 1964. Finally purchased outright by Union-Castle in 1974. Withdrawn April 1975. Thought to become a student hostel at Royal Albert Dock, London; never materialised. Instead, sold to Taiwan scrappers; broken-up at Kaohsiung during winter 1975–76.

Pendennis Castle

Service Mailship run from Southampton via Madeira or Las Palmas to Cape Town, Port Elizabeth, East London and Durban. **Particulars** 28,582 gross tons; 763 × 84 × 32 ft. **Builder** Harland & Wolff Limited, Belfast, Northern Ireland, 1958. **Machinery** Steam turbines, twin screw. Speed 22 knots. **Capacity** 197 first class, 473 tourist class, 66 interchangeable. **Notes** Laid down January 1956. Designed to make Southampton–Cape Town passage in 11½ days. Launched December 24 1957. Maiden voyage January 1959. Tonnage relisted as 28,453 in 1967 and again as 28,442 in 1972. Withdrawn June 1976 and sold to Far Eastern buyers. Owners listed as Ocean Queen Navigation Company, Panama flag. Ship re-named *Ocean Queen* and laid-up

A striking collection of views of the final three new Union-Castle liners at their Southampton berths. All are seen just prior to departing on their maiden voyages. The Pendennis Castle *(***below***); the* Windsor Castle (**top, following page**)*; and finally, the* Transvaal Castle (**bottom, following page**). (All Union-Castle).

Above *A telescopic view at Southampton's Western Docks of* (**from left to right**) *the* Oriana, S. A. Vaal, Pendennis Castle *and a Clan Line freighter* (Peter Smith collection).

at Hong Kong. Rumoured to become Middle Eastern hotel-ship; never materialised. Sold to Kinvarra Bay Shipping Company, Panama in 1977 and re-named *Sinbad I*. Continued in lay-up at Hong Kong. Moved to Kaohsiung, Taiwan in April 1980 for scrapping.

Windsor Castle

Service Mailship service to South Africa (same ports as for *Pendennis Castle*). **Particulars** 37,640 gross tons; 783 × 92 × 32 ft. **Builder** Cammell Laird & Company Limited, Birkenhead, England, 1960. **Machinery** Steam turbines, twin screw. Speed 23 knots. **Capacity** 237 first class and 585 tourist class (adjustable). **Notes** Largest liner ever built for the South African trade and largest Union-Castle liner. Launched by Queen Elizabeth, the Queen Mother on June 23 1959. Maiden voyage August 1960. Tonnage relisted as 36,123 in 1967 and then as 36,277. Final voyage to South Africa in August 1977. Withdrawn September 1977 and sold to John S. Latsis Line, Panama flag. Re-named *Margarita L.* Sailed Southampton to Piraeus in October 1977 and refitted as a hotel-ship. Arrived at Jeddah, Saudi Arabia in January 1979 for service as permanently moored hotel-ship Tonnage re-listed as 29,640.

Transvaal Castle/S. A. Vaal

Service Mailship run from Southampton via Madeira or Las Palmas to Cape Town, Port Elizabeth, East London and Durban. **Particulars** 32,697 gross tons; 760 × 90 × 32 ft. **Builder** John Brown & Company Limited, Clydebank, Scotland, 1961. **Machinery** Steam turbines, twin screw. Speed 22½ knots. **Capacity** 763 'hotel' class. **Notes** Terminated Union-Castle/ Safmarine passenger service. Launched January 17 1960. Maiden voyage January 1961. Transferred to management of South African Marine Corporation (Safmarine Lines) in January 1966. Re-named *S. A. Vaal* and repainted in Safmarine colours. Transferred to South African flag in 1969. Left Southampton on final Union-Castle/ Safmarine passenger sailing on September 2 1977.

Withdrawn from service October 1977. Sold to Carnival Cruise Lines, Panama flag. Rebuilt as a cruise-ship by Kawasaki Heavy Industries, Kobe, Japan. Given accommodation for 1,432 cruise passen-gers. Tonnage re-listed as 38,175. Re-named *Festivale.* Maiden Caribbean cruise from Miami in October 1978.

Above *The former* Transvaal Castle *in her Safmarine livery as the* S. A. Vaal (World Ship Society Photo Library).
Below *The same ship leaving Southampton for the last time in October 1977, now named the* Festivale *for the Carnival Cruise Lines and bound for a major refit in Japan* (Michael D. J. Lennon).

Bibliography

Bonsor, N. R. P., *North Atlantic Seaway*, Prescot, Lancashire: T. Stephenson & Sons Ltd, 1955.

Crowdy, Michael (editor), *Marine News* (journal), Kendal, Cumbria: World Ship Society, 1964–1984.

Dunn, Laurence, *British Passenger Liners*, Southampton: Adlard Coles Ltd, 1959.

Dunn, Laurence, *Passenger Liners*, Southampton: Adlard Coles Ltd, 1961.

Dunn, Laurence, *Passenger Liners* (revised edition), Southampton: Adlard Coles Ltd, 1965.

Eisele, Peter (editor), *Steamboat Bill* (journal), New York: Steamship Historical Society of America Inc, 1966–1984.

Kludas, Arnold, *Great Passenger Ships of the World, Volume 1–5,* Cambridge, England: Patrick Stephens Ltd, 1972–1974.

Kludas, Arnold, *The Great Passenger Ships & Cruise Liners of the World,* Herford, West Germany: Koehlers Verlagsgesellschaft GmbH, 1983.

Moody, Bert, *Ocean Ships*, London: Ian Allan Ltd, 1978.

Shopland, Robert (editor), *Ships Monthly* (journal), Burton-on-Trent, England: Waterway Productions Ltd, 1980–1984.

Vernon-Gibbs, C. R., *British Passenger Liners of the Five Oceans*, London: Putnam & Company Limited, 1963.

Yamada, Michio & Ikeda, Yoshiho, *Passenger Ships of the World,* Tokyo, 1981.

Index

Accra, 75
Activity, HMS, 83
Akarita, 120–21
Akaroa, 120
Amazon, 116
Amerikanis, 127
Amra, 38
Anchor Line, 21–2
Andes, 114–6
Anselm, 33–4
Apapa, 75
Aragon, 116
Aramac, 90
Aranda, 120
Arawa, 120–21
Arcadia, 102
Argentina Star, 32
Arlanza, 116
Aronda, 38
Athenic, 117
Athlone Castle, 124–5
Aureol, 76
Australasia, 33
Azure Seas, 118

Baudouinville, 32
Bibby Line, 22–5
Blue Funnel Line, 25–30
Blus Star Line, 30–32
Booth Line, 33–4
Borodino, 79
Braemar Castle, 127–8
Brasil Star, 32
Breconshire, 83
Britannic, 52
British India Steam Navigation Co, 34–48

Calabar, 74
Caledonia, 21–2
Calypso, 118
Camito, 76–7
Canadian Pacific Steamships, 48–51
Canberra, 103–6
Canton, 96
Capetown Castle, 124–5
Caribia, 64
Carinthia, 67
Carmania, 64–5
Carnarvon Castle, 122–3
Carnivale, 50
Caronia, 64
Carthage, 93
Cathay, 106–8
Centaur, 30
Ceramic, 117
Charon, 27
Chitral, 106–8
Chusan, 100–102
Cilicia, 21–2
Circassia, 21–2
City of Durban, 78
City of Exeter, 78
City of Port Elizabeth, 78
City of York, 78
Corfu, 93
Corinthic, 117
Cunard Adventurer, 71
Cunard Ambassador, 71
Cunard Countess, 72
Cunard Line, 51–72
Cunard Princess, 72
Curnow Shipping Ltd, 72

Dara, 38
Dardanus, 84
Daressa, 41
Denbighshire, 84
Derbushire, 23
Deucalion, 83
Devonia, 36
Devonshire, 23
Dominion Monarch, 116
Donaldson Line, 73
Duchess of Bedford, 49
Dumra, 38
Dunera, 36
Durban Castle, 124–5
Dwarka, 41

Edinburgh Castle, 126–7
Elder Dempster Lines, 74–6
Elders & Fyffes Ltd, 76–7
Ellerman & Bucknall Lines, 78–9
Ellerman's Wilson Line, 79
Empire Doon, 27
Empire Humber, 84
Empire Orwell, 27
Empress of Britain, 50
Empress of Canada, 50–51
Empress of England, 50
Empress of France, 48–50

Fairland, 67
Fairsea, 67
Fairwind, 67
Favorita, 47
Feodor Shalyapin, 65
Festivale, 131–3
Flavia, 62
Francis Drake, 82
Franconia, 64–5
Furness Bermuda Line, 80–81
Furness Warren Line, 82

George Anson, 82
Glen Line, 83–5
Glenartney, 83
Glenearn, 83
Glengarry, 84
Glengyle, 83
Glenorchy, 83
Glenroy, 84
Golden City, 74–5
Golden Lion, 74–5
Golfito, 76–7
Gorgon, 27
Gothic, 117
Gunung Djati, 27

Hania, 23–4
Hansa, 84
Hector, 27–30
Helenus, 27–30
Henderson Line, 86–7
Henrietta Latsi, 96
Heraklion, 25
Himalaya, 96
Höegh Transit, 120
Höegh Traveller, 120
Höegh Trotter, 120
Hubert, 33

Iberia, 102
Iberia Star, 32–3
Island Princess, 112–3
Island Venture, 112
Ivernia, 64–5
Ixion, 27–30

Jan Bakx, 22
Jason, 27–30

Kampala, 42
Kannon Maru, 23
Karanja, 42
Kareem, 42
Kengshin, 109
Kenya, 44
Kenya Castle, 127–8
Khaleej Express, 33
Kim Hwa, 41
Kri Tanjung Pandang, 27
Kungsholm, 109

Laurentia, 73
Leicestershire, 23–4
Leonid Sobinov, 65
Linda Clausen, 71
Lismoria, 73

Malaysia, 33
Mardi Gras, 51
Margarita L, 131
Marianna VI, 76
Marianna Latsi, 96
Mauretania, 56
Media, 62
Mediterranean Dolphin, 78
Mediterranen Island, 78
Mediterranean Sea, 78
Mediterranean Sky, 78
Mediterranean Sun, 78
Meersburg, 84
Mombasa, 42

Nancowry, 42
Nevasa, 48
New Zealand Shipping Co, 87–90
Newfoundland, 82
Northern Star, 118–20
Nova Scotia, 82

Ocean Monarch (Furness Bermuda), 80–82
Ocean Monarch, (Shaw Savill) 120–21
Ocean Queen, 128
Orcades, 98
Oriana, 102–3
Oriental Carnaval, 89
Oriental Esmeralda, 89
Oriental Rio, 90
Orion, 94–5
Oronsay, 98
Orontes, 91–2
Orsova, 98–100
Oxfordshire, 25

P&O-Orient Lines, 90–109
Pacific Princess, 112–3
Pacific Steam Navigation Co, 110
Paraguay Star, 32
Parthia, 62
Patroclus, 27
Peleus, 27
Pendennis Castle, 128–9
Perseus, 27
Phemius, 84
Philocteles, 27
Pretoria, 27
Pretoria Castle, 126–7
Priam, 83
Princess Cruises, 110–13
Prome, 86–7
Pyrrhus, 27

Queen Anna Maria, 50
Queen Elizabeth, 57–62
Queen Elizabeth 2, 68–9
Queen Mary, 52
Queen of Bermuda, 80–81

Rajula, 36
Rangat, 36
Rang, 89
Rangitane, 88–9
Rangitata, 86–7
Rangitiki, 86–8
Rangitoto, 88–9
Reina Del Mar, 110, 128–9
Remuera, 90
Rhodesia Castle, 127–8
Riviera, 82
Royal Mail Lines, 114–6
Royal Princess, 114
Ruahine, 89–90

S. A. Oranje, 126–7
S. A. Vaal, 131–3
St Helena, 72
Salween, 86–7
Sangola, 41
Santhia, 42
Sarpedon, 84
Saxonia, 64–5
Sea Princess, 109
Sea Venture, 112
Seawise University, 62
Seng Kong No. 1, 27
Shanghai, 109
Shaw Savill Line, 116–21
Sinbad I, 128–30
Sirdhana, 41
Sirius, 25
Southern Cross, 118
Spirit of London, 112
State of Haryana, 42
Strathaird, 95–6
Stratheden, 96
Strathmore, 96
Strathnaver, 95
Stirling Castle, 124–5
Sun Princess, 112
Sunward II, 72
Sylvania, 67

Tauphooshan, 75
Tamele, 74
Tarkwa, 74
Telemachus, 83
Thysville, 32
Transvaal Castle, 131–3

Uganda, 44
Umtali, 74
Umtata, 74

Union Castle Line, 122–32
Uruguay Star, 32

Varna, 81

Warwick Castle, 124–5
Warwickshire, 23
Winchester Castle, 122–4
Windsor Castle, 131
Winneba, 74
Worcestershire, 22